Fast Track to MDX

Springer
London
Berlin
Heidelberg
New York
Hong Kong
Milan
Paris
Tokyo

Fast Track to
MDX

Mark Whitehorn, Robert Zare
and Mosha Pasumansky

 Springer

Mark Whitehorn
University College Worcester, Worcester, UK

Robert Zare
Microsoft Corporation, Redmond, WA, USA

Mosha Pasumansky
Microsoft Corporation, Redmond, WA, USA

British Library Cataloguing in Publication Data
Whitehorn, Mark, 1953-
    Fast track to MDX
    1.OLAP technology 2.Data warehousing
    I.Title II.Zare, Robert III.Pasumansky, Mosha
    005.7'4
    ISBN 1852336811

Library of Congress Cataloging-in-Publication Data
A catalog record for this book is available from the Library of Congress

ISBN 1-85233-681-1 Springer-Verlag London Berlin Heidelberg
a member of BertelsmannSpringer Science+Business Media GmbH
Http://www.springer.co.uk

Typeset by Ian Kingston Editorial Services, Nottingham
Printed and bound at The Cromwell Press, Trowbridge, Wiltshire, England
34/3830-543210 Printed on acid-free paper SPIN 10887802

Contents

Foreword

I love Business Intelligence. I love BI because it is all about becoming better. BI is all about empowering us with knowledge and that knowledge is the power to realize our full potential. As Zorge the spy said, "knowledge is power", and who doesn't love to have the power to know, to understand and to make intelligent decision? I do.

Since the dawn of the modern information system it was obvious that the information accumulated in the machine is wasted if there is no way to analyze it and learn from it. From as early as the 1950s, data analysis systems and, later, decision support systems were designed, developed and deployed with that intent. However, only in the last decade have these systems become both reasonably affordable and mainstream and their business impact indisputable.

The last decade has also seen the emergence of OLAP as the centerpiece of the BI technologies. The OLAP multidimensional databases combine incredible performance with unsurpassed analytical power and, in my opinion, are the foundation of the BI platform.

While the performance differences between the multidimensional databases and the traditional relational databases are very significant, Moore's law, which states that the hardware computing power doubles every 18 months, renders this advantage of the OLAP databases temporary. Sooner or later, the raw computing power of the common server machines will be sufficient to provide the performance needed for sophisticated analysis even when the data is stored in a relational database.

However, where OLAP is likely to maintain a sustained advantage over the relational database is in its analytical capabilities. Here the differences are much deeper. The multidimensional data model is vastly superior to the relational data model when it comes to the expressiveness of analytical operations. The ability to have random access to any point in space, both detailed data and aggregates, makes it a breeze to express calculations that would otherwise take pages of SQL statements using a relational database.

This is also where MDX enters the picture and why MDX is so important. MDX is the way to express the analytics in the OLAP database. Without

MDX, all of the sophisticated calculations and smart analytics that we expect of OLAP technologies are simply impossible.

Moreover, by making MDX into an industry standard, the language has become the lingua franca of the BI world. Virtually every BI client application and almost all OLAP servers have adopted MDX as their primary if not exclusive query language. In a short period of 5 years MDX has become to multidimensional databases what SQL is to relational databases. Can you imagine where the technology of relational databases would have been today without having a common query language?

Undoubtedly, Microsoft's entrance into the BI market at the end of 1998 with the release of OLAP Services in SQL Server 7.0 was the most influential event in the young BI industry. Starting from early 1997 when I and the small Plato development team assembled in Building 6 on the Redmond campus our mission was clear: "BI to the masses." We were tasked with creating a very powerful yet easy to use OLAP Server that could be distributed and assimilated on a mammoth scale and with unprecedented low prices.

While we looked at every release as the most important product release and had high expectations from every one of the versions we shipped, it is clear to us that bringing BI to the masses is a long journey that will take almost a decade to complete. We have made huge progress in the four years since we shipped the first release of OLAP Services. SQL Server 7.0 shook all previously known conventions of ease of use and prices in OLAP products. Analysis Services in SQL Server 2000 captured the market share leadership and became the most widely deployed OLAP Server ever. We are very pleased with the accomplishments so far but we know that we still have some way to go before BI is truly available to the masses.

We are now working on a major new release of Analysis Services under the code name Yukon and by the time these lines are published some of the dramatic innovations in the product will be known to the public. I view Yukon as the release that will bring BI servers very close to the point of realizing the "BI for the masses" vision. MDX stays a critical component of the platform and we are making a huge investment to make it even more powerful as well as much easier to use. The power of MDX is the power of analytics and what makes BI so important.

Mosha Pasumansky is the development lead for the MDX engine of Analysis Services in Microsoft. Mosha and I go a long way back to the days when we both worked for Panorama Software. From the moment I saw the code that he produced it was clear to me that Mosha is a prodigy and was one of the finest developers I have ever seen. Mosha took over from me the responsibility for the calculation engine of the Panorama OLAP product and he has been doing multidimensional calculations ever since.

When Microsoft acquired Panorama and the development team relocated to Redmond in January 1997 Mosha joined a very small task force that was responsible for creating Tensor, the code name for the OLE DB for OLAP specification. As part of that effort we defined the central component of the standard – the MDX language. MDX carries a lot of Mosha's genes in it. For years Mosha has been an authority on the practical usages of MDX to solve common business and analytical problems. Reading a book about MDX by Mosha is reading a book from the guy who knows everything there is to know about MDX.

Rob Zare joined the team for the late phases of SQL 2000 release. Astonishingly, Rob joined us with almost no background in computing and was hired to do some of the grunt testing work of the product; testing the user interface to ensure that it was not defective in any obvious way. Very quickly we discovered that Rob possesses explosive energy and a unique desire to excel. While Rob was doing the grunt work during the day, superbly at that, he moonlighted at building some impressive OLAP applications using the technology and writing up a bunch of product improvement suggestions. Very quickly Rob caught the attention of some of the senior members of the team who started mentoring him in the various aspects of product design. Soon afterwards, Rob got a double promotion and was reassigned to the team as a "program manager," a position that in Microsoft means a person that designs and writes the product specifications.

Rob's expertise is in building usable systems. He is responsible for some of the key aspects of the user interface in the Yukon release and he designed major portions of the MDX authoring tools. I am incredibly impressed with Rob's work and when Yukon is released I am sure that when you look at the outstanding product design you'll agree with me. Rob's passion is in making hard things easy and when you read this book I am sure you'll appreciate that MDX is presented in an easy to digest form thanks to Rob's work.

Mark Whitehorn is the professional author of the trio. He is the one that took Mosha's and Rob's ideas and formed them into an easy to read and entertaining text. I am sure you'll enjoy his write up as much as I did.

To truly understand modern Business Intelligence and to harness the power of the OLAP platform one must understand MDX, and this book, written by some of the creators of MDX, goes a long way in bringing the reader into the MDX way of thinking.

Amir Netz
Product Unit Manager
SQL Server – Analysis Services
Microsoft Corp.

Introduction

This is where we try to convince you to buy the book and tell you what it tries to do and what it doesn't try to do. We also cover the housekeeping information such as introducing you to the sample files, pointing you to a web site for up-to-date information and generally setting the scene for the book. If you have already bought the book and/or know what it does, feel free to skip to Chapter 1 where the action starts. You can always come back later for the housekeeping information.

Why should you read this book?

OLAP (On-Line Analytical Processing) is an extremely potent tool and MDX (Multi-Dimensional eXpressions) is the key that unlocks the power of OLAP. If you have started to use Analysis Manager to create and/or use OLAP cubes then you'll rapidly reach the point where knowledge of MDX becomes useful, not to say essential. (OK, that's the major selling pitch over).

What is MDX?

Well, we suspect you have some kind of idea, otherwise the title of this book would not have attracted you, but for the record:

MDX is a language that allows you to query OLAP cubes in a way reminiscent of that in which SQL allows you to query relational databases. In addition MDX expressions (as they are called) can be used to add business logic to the cubes, to define simple and advanced security settings, to implement color coding for purposes of exception alerting, to create custom member roll-ups, custom level roll-ups, actions and so on – in other words, MDX is used almost everywhere in the design of effective OLAP cubes. If you build OLAP databases of any complexity then you are going to need MDX.

As an example, suppose that you have an OLAP cube that stores sales information – units sold, unit price, costs etc. – for different products in different stores. Study of this data alone can, of course, yield invaluable information but business users are likely to want to perform additional analysis using measures derived from the original data. They might, for example, ask for a measure that shows profit ((Units Sold × Unit Price) – Costs) and another that shows the percentage profit for each product. Then they might ask to see profit plotted as a year-to-date value. For more complex analyses they might want to see some of the measures plotted as moving averages, or perhaps the percentage change in revenue for every period when compared with the same period in the previous year.

Any and all of these can be added, on the fly, to existing cubes as what are called 'calculated measures'. Calculated measures are written in MDX.

Users can also ask for exceptional figures to be color coded (red for bad, green for good); they can even ask for the data in the cube to interact with the rest of their environment. For example, they might ask to be able to right click on the name of a particular store in the OLAP cube and then to have an option that will automatically fire up a browser and display a map showing the store's location.

All of this can be achieved with MDX, and everything described here and more is demonstrated in this book.

Who should read this book?

The obvious (and correct) answer is "you", assuming that you are an OLAP developer and/or a DBA, but our experience is that MDX is also invaluable for power OLAP users – that is, experienced business analysts.

In other words, it's aimed at anyone who has been involved with OLAP for some time and has hit situations where it is difficult to deliver what they, or their users, want and who is interested in getting more information out of their cubes.

Who are we?

Dr. Mark Whitehorn has been writing articles, white papers, columns and books about computing since 1987; his column in *Personal Computer World* is one of the longest-running database columns in the world. He specializes in database technology, data warehousing and OLAP and has written five books – two co-authored with Bill Marklyn, one of the original designers of Microsoft's Access. Their first book, *Inside Relational Databases*, is a best seller (at least, for a database book!) and is now in its second edition. On the academic side he is an honorary lecturer at the University of Dundee where he lectures on advanced data handling; he is also an associate senior research fellow at University College Worcester where he lectures and also manages the data warehouse team. On the more practical side he runs a consultancy company which specializes in database design and data warehousing. In his spare time he teaches a database design course and a data warehousing course for QA, the UK-based training and consultancy company.

In his spare, spare time he rebuilds old cars. The current project (nearly completed at the time of writing) is a car powered by a tank engine. For the next project, lurking in the barn, there lies an old aircraft engine....

Robert Zare has been working on the Analysis Services team since he joined Microsoft in 1999. Prior to joining Microsoft, he spent a bit of time working at a much less interesting company. Prior to this, he was attending school at the University of Washington and dreaming about someday working for Microsoft. He was originally a member of the Analysis Services test team where, amongst other things, he was responsible for reproducing customer production environments and finding nasty bugs in Mosha's code. During the past two years he has been working as a Program Manager responsible for the next generation of OLAP/MDX tools.

Mosha Pasumansky worked at Panorama Software Systems from its foundation in 1993 as a developer on the desktop OLAP product called Panorama. In 1996, Microsoft acquired the OLAP technology and development team from Panorama and Mosha became a developer in the Microsoft OLAP Services (later renamed Microsoft Analysis Services) team. In 1997, he was one of the authors of the OLEDB for OLAP specification which defined the MDX language. He also was the developer in charge for the first implementation of MDX in the Microsoft OLAP Services 7.0 product which shipped in 1998. In 2000 Mosha worked on the XML for Analysis specification and later became Microsoft's representative in the XML for Analysis council (www.xmla.org). In the XML/A council, among his other responsibilities, Mosha works in the MDXML work group. Currently he is the development lead of the Analysis Services engine team and he is working on the next version of Microsoft Analysis Services.

This book came about because I (Mark) attended Tech Ed, Microsoft's technical conference, at which Robert gave three excellent presentations on MDX. I got talking to him afterwards and the end result is this book which is based on those three talks. Somehow along the way we managed to get

Mosha involved in the project because we knew that as one of the initial authors of MDX, his help would be invaluable. And we were right.

Bugs (sorry – readware anomalies)

Since Mosha actually helped to design MDX, and Robert is a Program Manager responsible for OLAP/MDX tools, their knowledge of MDX can be assumed to be reasonably definitive. While we were working on this book, they supplied the sample files, the ideas and endless reams of helpful comments; my job was to turn all of that into a book. Ultimately any errors that appear are to be laid at my door because they will have been introduced during my attempts to translate Robert and Mosha's intimate knowledge of MDX into what we hope is a readable book. Apologies in advance.

If you happen across any bugs, I would be delighted if you would tell me by visiting www.penguinsoft.co.uk where all known problems (and fixes) will also be posted.

Acknowledgements

We are very grateful to the people at Microsoft who, as well as Robert and Mosha, originally contributed to the talks on which this book is based. They are:

Ariel Netz
Amir Netz
Thierry D'Hers

In addition, valuable proofreading work was carried out by Jane Hunt (University College Worcester), Irina Gorbach (Microsoft) and Aaron Johal (QA).

However, the person who contributed the most to the successful completion of this book was Mary Whitehorn who worked on it extensively, not only proof-reading the entire book (several times) but actually writing parts of it. You may wonder why she doesn't appear as an author – so do we, but it is her wish not ours: she is very modest.

What do we cover?

In order to use MDX effectively, you need to be familiar with concepts such as dimensions, measures, members, cells, hierarchies, aggregations, levels and member properties. Given your background you may well already be familiar with these, but we cover them in Chapter 1 just in case. We also cover tuples and sets, which may be familiar terms from relational database theory but have specific meanings in MDX.

In Chapters 2 to 4 we introduce MDX as a language and use MDX queries to illustrate the basic syntax. The real power of MDX lies in expressions, so they come next and, as the chapters progress, we gradually introduce you to more and more ways in which MDX can be used.

In fact, some of the later chapters contain a great deal of information and detail about Analysis Services with sometimes only a small amount of MDX coding. On the face of it this seems weird (given that this is a book on MDX) but in reality it is simply an excellent demonstration of the power of MDX. By the time we reach these chapters we are no longer teaching how to write basic MDX statements because by then you'll have acquired that skill. Instead we are trying to show you the enormous power that can be gained from using MDX effectively. In other words, it isn't how you write MDX that really counts: it's how, and where, you use it.

We have also tried to introduce MDX, not as an abstract computer language, but as a real tool that will help you to make your cubes work more effectively. (Indeed, the original talks on which this book was based were called "Using MDX to Solve Business Problems") so once we've introduced the syntax of MDX, we illustrate the language by using it to solve common business problems.

What we don't cover

Just in case we're giving the impression that this book does everything... it doesn't. We have tried to introduce you to MDX in the shortest possible time, but we have always kept in mind that, given the fact that you are reading a book on MDX, you are probably already a computer professional. So, for example, in Chapter 7 we introduce you to some of the numeric functions in MDX such as Sum, Count and Avg. We show you how to use them to provide a solution to a common problem and by the end of the book we've covered the eight most frequently used numeric functions. However, we won't be showing you how to use the other 27 numeric functions in MDX. For a start, some of them are relatively specialized, such as

StdevP which "returns the population standard deviation of a numeric expression evaluated over a set, using the biased population formula". But a more important point is that once you know how to use numeric functions in general you can always look up any extra ones that you need in the help system.

And it isn't just specific functions that we've left out. I guarantee that there is technical information that we know which we aren't going to tell you. As an example, at some stage we tell you that syntactically, members of a dimension can be referenced using square brackets, so a member called:

    Sales

can be referenced like this:

    [Sales]

What we aren't going to tell you is that if a member already has square brackets in its name, such as:

    Penguin [Penguinsson]

you don't just wrap it up in square brackets, you also have to add an extra closing square bracket like this:

    [Penguin [Penguinsson]]]

Why are we leaving you in the dark about this fascinating fact? Because it just adds clutter to the book. In many cases square brackets aren't essential when naming a member anyway. If you eventually hit the problem, your knowledge of MDX will (if we have done our work properly) enable you to interpret the error message, delve into the help system and solve the problem.

So, this isn't a complete reference to MDX; as the title tries to suggest, it is a fast track to learning MDX. It is designed to get you started quickly, and to give you the essential framework around which you can fill in the detail. Oh, and hopefully to show you that MDX is as easy to learn as any other language and to convince you that it is actually fun to use.

Disclaimer

While we have made every effort to ensure that the content of this book is accurate, we cannot take responsibility for any errors, glitches or disasters you may encounter in your experience of the products we cover. The variation between hardware, software, networking and communications renders it impossible to guarantee that something will work under all circumstances. Analysis Services and ProClarity run perfectly happily on a stand-alone PC and this would be our preferred platform for learning MDX. You can relax and experiment in an environment where there is no danger of damaging a production system.

The 'd' word

Data: singular or plural? We know, correctly speaking, that datum is singular and data is plural. We also know that it sounds funny when used that way so we've gone with common usage and, with apologies to purists, happily written "data is" throughout.

What's on the CD-ROM

Sample Files

We have made extensive use of examples throughout the book, and we encourage you to experiment with MDX rather than just read about it. To make this process much easier, we have included on the CD-ROM most of the sample OLAP cubes we used, as well as the data and the queries, expressions etc. Appendix 1 holds details of all these files, where they are and how to make use of them.

ProClarity

OLAP cubes are stores of data that can be managed, in Microsoft's case, by a tool called Analysis Manager. What Microsoft doesn't supply is a free graphical tool to allow end users to view and manipulate the data in an OLAP cube with MDX.

❛ *It is true that Microsoft supplies a sample MDX application.*

```
MDX Sample Application - MDXQuery.mdx                                    _ B X
File  Edit  Query  View  Help
 ◁  ☐ ☞ ☐  DB: FoodMart 2000  ▼  Queries: #1 select ‖  {[Measures].[Unit Sal...  ▼ ⬚ ⬚  ▷  ⬚⬚⬚ ⬚⬚ ⬚⬚  ⤤
select
   {[Measures].[Unit Sales]} on columns,
   order(except([Promotion Media].[Media Type].members,{[Promotion Media].[Media Type].[No Media]}),[Measures].[Unit Sales],DESC) on rows
from Sales

Cube:  Sales          ▼                                              Syntax Examples
 ⬡ Sales                                          ⊞ 🗀 (All)
 ⊞  ↳ Customers                                   ⊞ 🗀 Array
 ⊞  ↳ Education Level                             ⊞ 🗀 Dimension
 ⊞  ↳ Gender                                      ⊞ 🗀 Hierarchy
 ⊞  ↳ Marital Status                              ⊞ 🗀 Level
 ⊞  ↳ Measures                                    ⊞ 🗀 Logical
 ⊞  ↳ Product                                     ⊞ 🗀 Member

              Unit Sales
Daily Paper,   9,513.00
Daily Paper    7,738.00
Product Atta   7,544.00
Daily Paper,   6,891.00
Cash Regist    6,697.00
Sunday Pap     5,945.00
Street Hand    5,753.00
Sunday Pap     4,339.00
Bulk Mail      4,320.00
In-Store Cou   3,798.00
TV             3,607.00
Sunday Pap     2,726.00
Radio          2,454.00

⟁-DG
```

However, this really is just a sample application with no graphical capabilities; you are unlikely to be cruel enough to inflict it on real users. ❜

With that in mind, we have provided on the CD-ROM a time-limited version of ProClarity, which is just such a front-end tool. It comes with an excellent graphical interface that allows users with zero knowledge to browse and manipulate the data in an OLAP cube.

In addition, if you select View, MDX Editor from the main menu, you can see the MDX that ProClarity is using to generate the current view of the data. Even better, you can use this editor to create new MDX statements, or indeed to cut and paste in the ones we have provided for you in the text files.

We think that ProClarity is an excellent tool for business users and also an excellent tool to help you to learn MDX. Indeed, we've used it to illustrate the book, and as a visualization tool to show you the effects of different MDX queries and expressions. However, this does not mean that it is obligatory for you to load and use ProClarity to understand the contents of the book.

In order to work through the examples, it is clearly essential to have a front-end tool of some kind. If you are already using one that you like, we'd recommend that you continue to use that. If not, we recommend that you install ProClarity Professional and see how you get on with it.

Appendix 2 contains further details about installing and running ProClarity.

Chapter 1

Readme.doc – definitions you need to know

Sample data

We used a sample set of data and a sample cube in order to produce the screen shots that appear in this chapter. However, the cube was created just to provide the screen shots and has very little merit as a real cube so we haven't, therefore, included it on the CD-ROM.

Italics

One of the problems inherent in writing a book like this is the need to tread a thin line between defining terms in a readable way and ensuring that we are as precise as possible. Sometimes we've tried to do this by giving a general overview of a term and then giving a more formal definition. At other times, we have felt that even a general description needs to be qualified. In those cases we have often put the further qualifications in italics. Anything that you find in italics can be read as an aside to the main discussion and it should be possible to skip the italics on your first read through and still get the overall picture.

❛ *In fact, this applies as a general rule throughout the book. The comments in italics are asides to the general information.* ❜

Introduction

We are going to use this chapter to define many of the terms that are used in MDX. These will include:

- Dimensions
- Measures
- Members
- Cells
- Hierarchies
- Aggregations
- Levels
- Tuples
- Sets
- Member Properties

We briefly considered creating a glossary and defining each term individually, but it is difficult to maintain a sense of context in a glossary because all of the entries have to stand alone. So instead we will describe the factors that affect how a cube is constructed and use that to introduce the definitions as we go along.

If you have been building OLAP cubes for any length of time, the definitions of the first few terms are likely to be already firmly embedded into your brain. If so, simply fast forward until you hit one that you don't know. If that means you end up jumping to Chapter 2, that's fine.

What happens if you aren't familiar with the terms? Well, the obvious answer is to read through this entire chapter, making sure that you understand all the terms before moving on to the actual coding. That works fine for some people but it can work really badly for others. The 'others' are those who want to get started, now! They want to feel a keyboard working under their finger tips. They want to type code in, try it, see it fail, modify it, try it again, get it working. If they then hit a term that they don't understand, they are happy to divert for a little background reading. We've written this chapter, therefore, assuming that it will be read from beginning to end. But we've also tried to write it in a reasonably modular way so that you can jump straight to Chapter 2 and get started and flip back when you need a definition. The terms appear in the order listed above and there are headings to guide you, so you can scan through the chapter until you see the one you want.

Dimensions, measures, members and cells

OLAP cubes are stores of multi-dimensional data. MDX is all about manipulating OLAP cubes so in order to understand why MDX works in the way it does, it is an excellent idea to get a firm grip on the way in which multi-dimensional data is described, stored and defined.

An OLAP cube is made up of **Dimensions** and **Measures**. In the figure below, there are two dimensions, Time and Product. The Product dimension has four **Members** – Sardines, Anchovies, Herrings and Pilchards. The Time dimension also happens to have four members (April to July). There is one measure, UnitsSold, which is simply the number of cans of each product sold in each month.

For this two-dimensional 'cube' you can think of the members of the product dimension as being the labels for the columns of a worksheet. The members of the time dimension then form the labels of the rows and the values of the measure appear in the **Cells**.

UnitsSold

	Product			
Time	Sardines	Anchovies	Herrings	Pilchards
April	16	23	12	4
May	14	12	23	6
June	34	19	19	8
July	17	22	14	4

You can, of course, reverse the rows and columns without disrupting the meaning of the data.

UnitsSold

	Time			
Product	April	May	June	July
Sardines	16	14	34	17
Anchovies	23	12	19	22
Herrings	12	23	19	14
Pilchards	4	6	8	4

Clearly, each cell can be described in terms of one member from each dimension – thus we can see that the number of anchovies sold in June was 19. We could say more formally that each value for the measure UnitsSold occurs at a unique intersection between two members from the different dimensions.

❢ *Expressing it in this way imparts exactly the same information, you just get more street cred. for knowing the jargon.* ❟

It is easy for humans to visualize a cube like this that consists of two dimensions and a single measure. There is no reason, however, why a cube should be limited to one measure. As well as the unit sales figures shown above, you might also want to store, say, profit. There are several ways in which we can represent (and you can visualize) this. You might be happy picturing it like this:

UnitsSold/Profit

	Product			
Time	Sardines	Anchovies	Herrings	Pilchards
April	16 $40.00	23 $78.20	12 $23.88	4 $8.20
May	14 $35.00	12 $40.80	23 $45.77	6 $12.30
June	34 $85.00	19 $64.60	19 $37.81	8 $16.40
July	17 $42.50	22 $74.80	14 $27.86	4 $8.20

with the UnitsSold figure occupying the left of the cell and the profit occupying the right.

Alternatively, you could think of each measure represented by a single worksheet in a spreadsheet application, so you end up with a stack of sheets showing the same dimensions but different measures, like this:

UnitsSold

	Product			
Time	Sardines	Anchovies	Herrings	Pilchards
April	16	23	12	4
May	14	12	23	6
June	34	19	19	8
July	17	22	14	4

Profit

	Product			
Time	Sardines	Anchovies	Herrings	Pilchards
April	$40.00	$78.20	$23.88	$8.20
May	$35.00	$40.80	$45.77	$12.30
June	$85.00	$64.60	$37.81	$16.40
July	$42.50	$74.80	$27.86	$8.20

The way you choose doesn't matter too much; the important thing is to understand that a cube can have multiple measures – within reason as many as you want.

❝ *OK, so you want exact figures. A cube in Analysis Services can have up to 1,024 measures. For the record it can also have up to 128 dimensions, each with potentially thousands or millions of members.* ❞

As well as multiple measures, cubes can also have more than two dimensions. Suppose that our company has multiple stores and we want to see the UnitsSold figures broken down for individual stores. No problem, we just add another dimension, called Store, to contain the information about our outlets, looking like this:

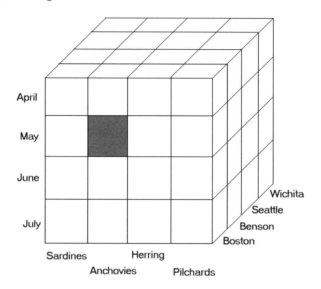

(We've cut back to a single measure for this cube, just to keep the diagram relatively simple.)

The cell that's highlighted in the cube above sits at an intersection of the cube's three axes and each axis represents a dimension. The shaded cell lines up with anchovies from the Product dimension (the x axis), May from the Time dimension (the y axis) and Boston from the Store dimension (the z axis). The value that we would find in this cell tells us the number of anchovies sold in May in our Boston store.

Visualizing three dimensions is also relatively easy; we live in a three-dimensional world and so we're quite good at three-dimensional concepts. However, OLAP cubes can have many more dimensions.

In our example, there could be an Employee dimension to tell us which member of staff made the sales, and a Customer dimension indicating to whom the sales were made. That's five dimensions already. This is a good time to stop trying the visualizations: mental pictures of two- and three-dimensional data are excellent for building a basic understanding of what OLAP cubes are all about but once we exceed three dimensions, it's much easier to rely on words rather than pictures.

Talking about values in a five-dimensional cube turns out to be perfectly straightforward: in May, our man Steve in the Boston store sold five cans of anchovies to Katie for a profit of $12.50. In that simple sentence we used all five dimensions (Time, Employee, Store, Product and Customer). We also slipped in not one but two measures: UnitsSold (five cans of anchovies) and Profit ($12.50).

However, as long as we keep the number of dimensions and measures down to reasonable levels for the rest of this chapter, diagrams are still really useful to help explain the terms used in OLAP cubes and hence in MDX.

Cranking up the complexity

So far we have built up a set of words (Dimensions, Measures, Members, Cells) and definitions that allow us to describe simple OLAP cubes. Do we have to make it any more complex? Yes, because this is still too simple a model for the sort of analysis that business users actually want to achieve. Analysts and business people typically want to query their data in much more complex ways and so OLAP cubes have to be capable of handling that complexity. For instance, UnitsSold totals for each month of trading might be required, or totals for each quarter of the current year, or even totals for each year.

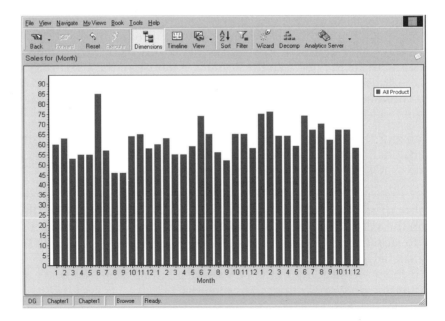

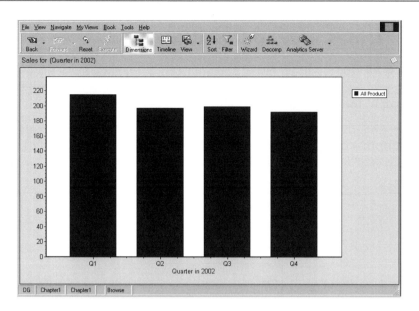

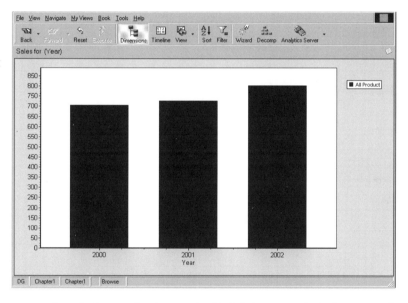

Our current level of complexity can't do this because it only caters for one unit type of member in each dimension – for example, we can only represent months in the time dimension. In order to give users rapid access to data totaled in this way, these quarterly and yearly totals need to be stored in the OLAP cube as well. This in turn means that we need to handle some of the dimensions as what are called **hierarchies**.

Hierarchies and aggregations

While there is no obligation for all dimensions in a cube to be hierarchical, experience suggests that many are in practice. Most cubes have a time dimension, for example, and time is almost always hierarchical.

We can imagine the different totals – those for each year, each quarter and each month – being held in worksheet-like grids. The total item `UnitsSold` for each year for, say, the Boston store might look like this:

UnitsSold

		Product			
Time		Sardines	Anchovies	Herrings	Pilchards
Year	2000	242	199	196	65
	2001	232	201	219	75
	2002	294	214	209	86

and for quarter, like this:

UnitsSold

		Product			
Time		Sardines	Anchovies	Herrings	Pilchards
Quarter	Q1	61	36	58	21
	Q2	64	54	54	18
	Q3	45	59	33	12
	Q4	72	50	51	14

and like this for each month:

UnitsSold

		Product			
Time		Sardines	Anchovies	Herrings	Pilchards
Month	April	16	23	12	4
	May	14	12	23	6
	June	34	19	19	8
	July	17	22	14	4

We could also represent these values in a rather more complex grid like this:

			Sardines	Anchovies
2000	Q3	July	17	22
		Aug	16	18
		Sept	12	19
	Q3 total		45	59
2000	Q4	Oct	27	19
		Nov	24	19
		Dec	21	12
	Q4 total		72	50
2000 total			242	199

These representations of what is going on inside a cube are, as you can see, storing values derived by adding up, or aggregating, the original data in the cube. In practice, aggregations are not the only values that can be calculated from the original data – for example, a cube can also hold values expressed as percentages. However, no matter how they are calculated, such values are usually referred to as **aggregations**.

In fact, the term aggregation is very useful when discussing cubes, but it isn't one that is directly used in MDX. Aggregations are just an optimization that the underlying storage engine uses to speed up the response of the cube. The presence or absence of aggregations doesn't change any of the results of MDX expressions or queries.

In order to help us discuss hierarchies, it is useful to introduce the term **Level**.

Levels

Staying with a Time dimension, its hierarchy might look like this:

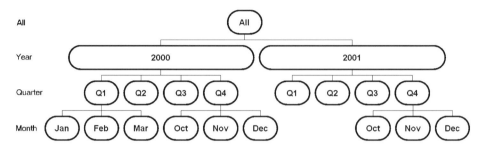

(In order to keep the diagram readable, only some of the members of the month level are shown.)

Just as ogres have layers (see Shrek), hierarchies have levels. In the example above, the Time dimension has four levels: All, Year, Quarter and Month. Year, Quarter and Month are just as you'd expect and All is simply a handy means of giving access to all the time data stored in the cube, for producing the answer to questions like "what is the total number of items sold for the period covered by data in the cube?" Most hierarchical dimensions have an All level at the top.

The top of a hierarchy is always the level that encompasses the greatest amount of information in the smallest number of members. Thus All is at the top of the hierarchy and you read 'down' that hierarchy to Month at the bottom. Or you can start with Month at the bottom (or 'leaf' level) and read 'up' to All at the top.

A leaf level is the level that's at the bottom of a branch of the hierarchy, and the term leaf node is used to mean a member of that leaf level. The leaf analogy comes from the branching, tree-like shape of a hierarchy, albeit a tree that's upside-down.

Levels have members, and a member is a single item in a dimension. It will sit at one of the levels in the dimension's hierarchy. To continue with the Time dimension example, at the Year level, you might have members called 2000, 2001 and 2002. At the Quarter level, there are likely to be members called something like Q1, Q2, Q3 and Q4 and so on.

As we've said, most dimensions are hierarchical – take the Store dimension, for example. Stores could be grouped together into states so that analysis can be performed between individual stores and also between different states.

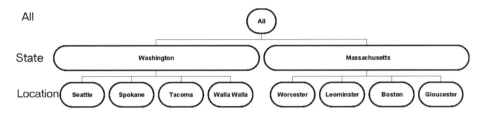

Naming conventions

Now we know that there are levels in a hierarchy and that each level has a descriptive name, like All, State and Location in the diagram above. We also know that each level contains members: Seattle and Leominster are members of the Location level. What good does this information do us? Well, once we start writing MDX code, we'll need a way of identifying precisely the specific members with which we want the code to work.

The most obvious way to identify a member is to start with the name of the dimension and work downwards, specifying the members at each level in the hierarchy until we reach required member. Working with the Store dimension shown in the diagram above, we'd indicate the Leominster member like this:

```
[Store].[All].[Massachusetts].[Leominster]
```

This is, in fact, the method we will be using almost everywhere in this book. It has the advantage of precision which outweighs its tendency towards the verbose.

There is a temptation, however, to take short cuts with these long path names. It's clear that in our simple example above, we could use just the dimension name and then go straight to the name of the member we want, like this:

```
[Store].[Leominster]
```

to point unequivocally to the Leominster member. This works here, but such short cuts will only work with certain data and with certain naming conventions.

If you look back at the diagram that shows the hierarchy of the Time dimension, you'll see that there will be two Octobers, one in 2000 and one in 2001. Here we couldn't take a short cut like:

    [Time].[October]

and be sure we were pointing to exactly the right member.

With some dimensions it is relatively easy to impose a naming convention that uses unique member names and is therefore amenable to the use of short cuts. For example, the Time dimension could be re-structured so that the members at the Quarter level were called 2000-Q1, 2001-Q2 and so on, and the members at the Month level were called October-2000, May-2001 etc. The gain is that you can then reference them simply by dimension name and unique member name:

    [Time].[June-2001]

rather than:

    [Time].[All].[2001].[Q2].[June].

❛ *It seems only fair to point out that we can do this because we are using sample data. In reality you can still be caught out by real data because there are cases where even full path names don't help. For example, suppose that you discover that there are two places called Leominster in the state of Massachusetts. In that case even a full path name:*

    [Store].[All].[Massachusetts].[Leominster]

wouldn't distinguish between them.

This type of duplication is all too frequent in real data. English counties (which are far smaller than US states) are littered with duplicates: there are two places called Ashton in Cornwall, for example.

In order to solve this problem Analysis Services provides a means of identifying members by means of their 'member keys' rather than by their member names – there's more about this in Chapter 14. ❜

It is worth noting that, despite appearances, client tools such as ProClarity, Excel etc. don't themselves ever create the names of the members that they subsequently use in the MDX expressions or queries that they generate. In fact, these tools are explicitly warned not to do so by the OLEDB for OLAP specification. Instead, the server generates the unique names for them, and it has all kinds of rules about how it can do this. Sometimes the server will generate a name of the type that we have already discussed here – dimension.name.name.name. For example:

```
[Store].[All].[Washington].[Tacoma]
```

However, it can also be in the form dimension.level.name, for example:

```
[Store].[Location].[Tacoma]
```

or even sometimes something completely different. As far as the tools are concerned, they never try to make sense out of the names. Instead they let the user point and click to the objects they want in the interface and the tool uses the names it has been given for those objects to generate the MDX that is then sent back to the server as a query or an expression. Hand-written MDX, on the other hand, can use whatever the person writing it feels like at the time. As a general rule we recommend using fully qualified names, such as dimension.name.name.name.name.

Tuples and sets

We need to define these terms accurately because they are of fundamental importance to an understanding of MDX. In later chapters you are going to meet expressions and functions that require you to give them, very specifically, a set or a tuple. However, we are quite well aware that defining the terms 'Tuple' and 'Set' has caused problems in the past; at least with reference to MDX.

Part of the problem is that, although these terms can be defined very accurately and succinctly in mathematical terms, defining them in more human terms tends to lead to very impenetrable definitions. This is because human language is so imprecise when compared to mathematics.

What we are going to do is to define them several times. The first definitions won't be totally accurate but will hopefully give a good feel for the important distinctions between tuples and sets. Then we'll add some more information and use examples to fill in some of the finer detail.

Tuples

❝ *We'll go back to the simple three-dimensional model with a single measure that we used earlier.* ❞

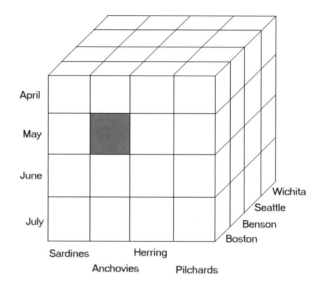

The highlighted cell sits at an intersection of the cube's three axes and each axis represents a dimension. The cell lines up with Anchovies from the Product dimension (the x axis), May from the Time dimension (the y axis) and Boston from the Store dimension (the z axis). The value that we would find in this cell tells us the number of anchovies sold in May in our Boston store.

We can express this description of the cell more neatly in pseudo-MDX as:

```
([Product].[Anchovies],[Time].[May],[Store].[Boston])
```

Here we are using the names of three members to point to the cell. In fact, the order in which we list the members is immaterial; we could equally well point to the cell like this:

```
([Product].[Anchovies],[Store].[Boston],[Time].[May])
```

Either way, we have a precise and unequivocal description of the location of the cell in the OLAP cube. In essence what we have done here is to identify a cell using its co-ordinates. The co-ordinates are members – one taken from each of the three dimensions. The name for this collection of co-ordinates is a **tuple**.

It is important to distinguish here between the tuple and the cell contents. One way to do so is to try to find an analogy from a more familiar system – a spreadsheet.

	A	B	C
1	12	32	45
2	37	23	12
3	65	45	32
4	78	56	44
5	98	23	34
6	290	179	167

In this worksheet, cell C4 contains the value 44. The value is located at the intersection of C and 4. So 44 is the value that the cell contains and "C4" is the spreadsheet equivalent of a tuple in an OLAP cube.

❢ *So how are you supposed to pronounce 'tuple'? Answer – whatever. Arguments rumble on as to whether it rhymes with couple or pupil. It's possible that the former is more common in the US and the latter favored in the UK. The Brits would argue that, if it rhymes with couple, it should be spelt tupple. The Americans would counter with "OK, but if it rhymes with pupil, why isn't it spelt tupil?" In my opinion the only certainty is that anyone both loud and confident about the 'correct' pronunciation is wrong.* ❢

Since a tuple points to a single cell, it follows inexorably that each member in the tuple has to be from a different dimension. To put that another way, you can never have a tuple which has two or more members taken from a single dimension. Why not? Well, if you do, it is inevitable that the 'tuple' that you create will end up pointing to more than one cell. For example:

```
(([Product].[Anchovies],[Time].[May],[Store].[Boston]),
([Product].[Sardines],[Time].[May],[Store].[Boston]))
```

has two members from the Product dimension and therefore can't be a tuple because it is pointing to more than one cell, as the following diagram shows.

So a first definition of a tuple could be:

A tuple is the intersection of one (and only one) member taken from each of the dimensions in the cube. A tuple identifies a single cell in the multi-dimensional matrix.

Sets

Given the above definition of a tuple, a set becomes very easy to define because a set is simply a collection of tuples which have been defined using the same dimensions.

What do we mean by 'defined using the same dimensions'? Well, take these two tuples.

```
([Product].[Anchovies],[Time].[May],[Store].[Boston])
([Product].[Sardines],[Time].[May],[Store].[Boston])
```

Both have exactly one member from the Time, Store and Product dimensions, so they have been defined using the same dimensions.

❝ *In fact, we can say that they have the same 'dimensionality'.* ❞

So these two tuples, taken together, form a set. Although we go into the exact syntax in Chapter 4, it is worth knowing at this point that in practice, the set has to be wrapped up in curly braces like this:

```
{([Product].[Anchovies],[Time].[May],[Store].[Boston]),
([Product].[Sardines],[Time].[May],[Store].[Boston])}
```

So we can define a set like this:

A set is a collection of tuples with the same dimensionality.

In essence this definition is saying that a set is simply a collection of tuples; nothing too complicated there. However, in the interests of accuracy we need to extend the definition slightly because, as it stands, this definition **implies** that a set always has to contain two or more tuples. While that is often the case, it is also true that the collection of tuples in a set can also be one tuple or even zero tuples.

This may sound weird at first. You may want to ask "But if a set contains only a single tuple, doesn't that make the set a tuple?" You might even want to ask "How can a set possibly contain no tuples?" These are both fair questions.

The answer is that one of the reasons for defining sets in the first place is that some MDX expressions are built to expect multiple tuples. For example, there is a function called AVG (which appears in Chapter 7) which will work out averages for you. Clearly, you usually want to average more than one value so the AVG function expects to be passed a set rather than a tuple (in fact, it demands to be passed a set). However, we also want it to work under conditions when it is passed a tuple (which will point to a single cell) and even when it is passed an empty set. So the function is designed to expect a set, and a set is defined as being a collection of zero, one or more tuples. This means that our first definition can be extended to read as follows:

A set is a collection of tuples with the same dimensionality. It may have more than one tuple, but it can also have only one tuple, or even have zero tuples, in which case it is an empty set.

So, to summarize so far:

- A tuple points to a single cell, and cannot include more than one member from any particular dimension.
- A set is a collection of tuples.

Exploring the differences between tuples and sets

OK, given the definitions that we currently have, and bearing in mind that we are still using pseudo MDX, is the following a tuple or a set?

```
([Time].[May], [Store].[Boston], [Product].[Anchovies])
```

Answer – a tuple.

OK, now what about these two?

```
1 ([Store].[Boston], [Product].[Anchovies])
2 {([Time].[April], [Store].[Boston], [Product].[Anchovies]),
   ([Time].[May], [Store].[Boston], [Product].[Anchovies]),
   ([Time].[June], [Store].[Boston], [Product].[Anchovies]),
   ([Time].[July], [Store].[Boston], [Product].[Anchovies])}
```

Well, one big clue is that we have wrapped curly braces around the second one, but ignoring those briefly, it is worth trying to work out in your own mind the differences and similarities between these two.

We could argue that both are pointing to the same collection of cells in the cube:

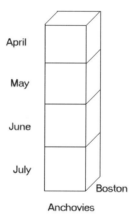

The first statement:

```
([Store].[Boston], [Product].[Anchovies])
```

is made up of two members, one from the Store dimension and the other from the Product dimension. Since it doesn't give us any information about the third dimension, we will (for the present) assume no restriction for that dimension.

The second statement:

```
{([Time].[April], [Store].[Boston], [Product].[Anchovies]),
 ([Time].[May], [Store].[Boston], [Product].[Anchovies]),
 ([Time].[June], [Store].[Boston], [Product].[Anchovies]),
 ([Time].[July], [Store].[Boston], [Product].[Anchovies])}
```

actively points to the four cells shown above.

So, as we have said, the two appear to be pointing to the same set of cells. However, the first statement **is** a tuple, the second **is** a set. How can we be so sure?

Well, the second statement is clearly a set because even our simple definition of set tells us that "A set is a collection of tuples with the same dimensionality". This statement has four tuples. Each of these four tuples has exactly one member from the Time, Store and Product dimensions, so these tuples have the same dimensionality. Therefore it is clearly a set.

The first statement conforms to part of the definition of a tuple, the bit that reads "A tuple is the intersection of several members each taken from a different dimension in the cube."

It describes the intersection of two members and each is taken from a different dimension. However, it appears to be failing the first part of our definition, the bit about "A tuple always identifies a single cell in the multi-dimensional matrix." But appearances can be deceptive!

And this is crunch time, this is where people have trouble with the definition of a tuple. So, let's be quite clear about what we are trying to say. This:

```
([Store].[Boston], [Product].[Anchovies])
```

is a tuple. The over-riding reason that we know it is a tuple is because it doesn't use more than one member from the same dimension. This may sound like a very fine distinction, but it isn't.

Think about it this way. Suppose that you have a three-dimensional cube like this:

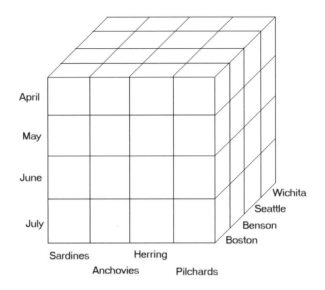

You then define one member from a dimension, say:

```
([Product].[Anchovies])
```

With that one statement you have trimmed the cube down to this:

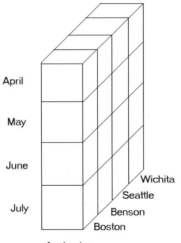

Adding another member from another dimension further trims the cube:

```
([Product].[Anchovies],[Store].[Boston])
```

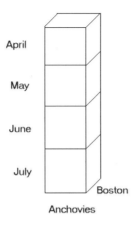

Each time you add another member from another dimension you are further refining what you want from the cube and, if you choose enough members, each from a different dimension, you will inevitably end up with a single cell.

Now suppose that we start off with this:

```
([Store].[Boston], [Store].[Seattle])
```

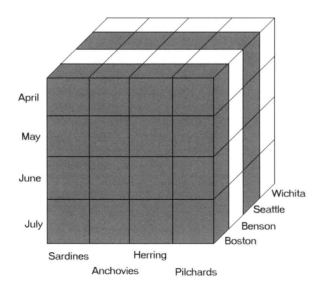

Once again we have only used a single dimension to restrict the cells in which we are interested, but already we are inevitably committed to ending up with a set rather than a tuple, and the reason why that is so is hopefully becoming clearer. No matter what members we use from the other dimensions, and even if we use members from every available dimension, we are going to end up with more than one cell because we started with more than one member from a given dimension.

So even if we restrict this with one member from each of the other two dimensions:

```
([Store].[Boston], [Store].[Seattle],([Time].[April],
[Product].[Anchovies])
```

we still end up with two cells:

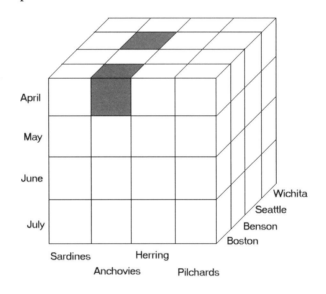

So, as we said earlier, this:

```
([Store].[Boston], [Product].[Anchovies])
```

is a tuple. We know it is a tuple, not because it currently points to a single cell, but because it doesn't use more than one member from the same dimension and therefore has the potential to point to a single cell.

Tuples don't have to use a member from every dimension

Now, in case this is making it all sound too complicated, we haven't actually changed the original definition of tuple very much. Initially we said:

A tuple is the intersection of one (and only one) member taken from each of the dimensions in the cube. A tuple identifies a single cell in the multi-dimensional matrix.

This definition assumes that we are defining a tuple using one member from every dimension. If we do use one member from every dimension it is inevitable that our tuple will identify just one single cell. But we don't have to use a member from **every** dimension.

So now we are refining that definition to read as:

A tuple is the intersection of one (and only one) member taken from one or several of the dimensions in the cube. A tuple identifies (or has the potential to identify) a single cell in the multi-dimensional matrix.

We are sticking to the original point that a tuple is always defined by a single member from any given dimension; all we are dropping is the requirement that you have to use each and every dimension to define the tuple.

So the following are all tuples:

```
[Product].[Anchovies],[Time].[May],[Store].[Boston]
[Product].[Anchovies],[Time].[May]
[Product].[Anchovies]
[Time].[May]
[Product].[Anchovies],[Store].[Boston]
```

But do these tuples still point to a single cell?

Yes, because all dimensions have what can be considered to be a 'default member'. So if in an MDX query you don't specify a member for a particular dimension, then the default member for that dimension is implied.

So, if this tuple were used in a query:

```
([Store].[Boston], [Product].[Anchovies])
```

a 'default member' will be used from each of the missing dimensions, effectively turning the tuple into something like this:

```
([Store].[Boston], [Product].[Anchovies],[Time].[May])
```

to ensure that the tuple does point to a single cell.

❦ *So, where does the 'default member' come from? In practice, MDX will use the so-called current member (which may be the default member if the user has not sliced the data). We only mention this here for completeness; when we introduce queries and expressions in later chapters, this will hopefully make more sense.* ❧

The take-home message from all of this is that you often don't have to use a member from every dimension when specifying a tuple.

Tuples and hierarchies

Next, it is worth discussing how tuples work with hierarchies.

Suppose that our cube has a hierarchical structure for Time. We have levels called Month, Quarter and Year and we have data for the years 1999, 2000 and 2001.

Is a pseudo-MDX expression like this:

```
([Product].[Anchovies],[Store].[Boston],[Time].[2000])
```

still a tuple? The acid test is "Does it still point to a single cell?" The answer is that it does because we have an aggregation member called 2000 and so somewhere in the cube there will be a single cell that holds the value for the total number of anchovies sold in Boston during the year 2000.

❦ *You may well be aware that when you create a real cube not all of the aggregations are necessarily pre-calculated. So you might begin to think "If the aggregation has not been pre-calculated, does this affect whether this is a tuple?" Again it is a good question; the answer is that this is still a tuple. Think of it this way. In MDX a cell is considered to be an intersection of a set of co-ordinates, not a physical object. Therefore aggregated cells **always** exist, because the intersections of the co-ordinates always exist. Some cells will be materialized (that is they will already have been calculated and stored) and some cells will have to be computed on the fly, but they always exist as far as MDX is concerned.* ❧

Sometimes measures behave like dimensions

What happens if we have essentially the same cube but with three measures, say UnitsSold, Profit and Price? Well, it doesn't make too much difference because the measures are going to act, in this case, pretty much like a dimension with three members.

So, we can specify the measure we want in just the same way as we specify a member from a dimension:

```
([Product].[Anchovies],[Store].[Boston],[Time].[May],
[Measures].[Profit])
```

Again, if you don't specify the measure, the expression will use the default measure (these are discussed at the end of Chapter 10).

So be aware that sometimes you'll hear people talking about measures as if they are dimensions. For example, "Try that query again, but this time use the UnitsSold member from the measures dimension." This is perfectly normal and, when you think about it, makes perfect sense. In fact, it explains why some of the GUI tools used to manipulate OLAP cubes show the measures as just another dimension.

Tuples revisited

So, hopefully, we've managed to convince you that a tuple is a relatively easy concept but just for completeness, here is a more formal definition.

A tuple is defined as an intersection of exactly a single member from each dimension (hierarchy) in the cube. For each dimension (hierarchy) that is not explicitly referenced, the current member is implicitly added to the tuple definition. A tuple always identifies (or has the potential to identify) a single cell in the multi-dimensional matrix. That could be an aggregate or a leaf level cell, but nevertheless one cell and only one cell is ever implied by a tuple.

Sets revisited

Our earlier definition of set:

A set is a collection of tuples with the same dimensionality. It may have more than one tuple, but it can also have only one tuple, or even have zero tuples, in which case it is an empty set.

still stands up to reasonable scrutiny.

Measures revisited

As we said when talking about tuples, there are times when we treat measures as if they were dimensions, and this is perfectly valid. However, in case this leaves you with the impression that there is no difference, it seems worth stressing how measures and dimensions do differ.

For a start, measures are frequently numerical and, equally frequently, those numbers are continuously variable (they can contain any possible numerical value between two limits). Sales figures, prices, gross profit – all these values come from a continuously variable range of numbers.

Measures have special properties attached to them, for example Data Type, Format String etc.

Finally, measures are not hierarchical.

Dimensions, on the other hand, are typically character-based and the values they contain are often discontinuously variable (the level Year can contain 2001 and 1999 but not 1999.5).

Member properties

So, is all continuously variable data likely to end up as a measure? In the main, the answer is 'yes', but keep an eye out for exceptions. There are some pieces of data that look at first glance like just the sort of data you'd store as a measure. Take a value such as the floor area of each store: each value will be continuously variable and numeric, so it's a measure, right? Well, no.

Think about a measure – it is stored at the intersection of the members of the dimensions in the cube. Suppose that the Boston store has a floor area of 21,000 sq. ft. If we enter this as a measure, at the intersection of Boston, Q1 and Anchovies we'll have a value of 21,000. At the intersection of Boston, Q2 and Anchovies we'll find the value 21,000. And at Boston, Q3, Herrings... we'll find... err... 21,000 again. In other words, the value we have for floor area doesn't depend at all on the Time dimension or on the Product dimension. But measures are supposed to depend on all of the dimensions. So the bottom line is that a measure is not the appropriate place to store data like a store's floor area, nor for any data that depends upon the member in only one dimension for its value.

What do we do instead? Members have **Properties** and the role of a property is to hold information about a member. Our floor area data fits into this category beautifully: it is information about one particular member. In this case, each member is a store and each store's floor area is a piece of information that has relevance only to that particular store.

Summary

If you are new to this whole dimensional data business, there's a great deal of new information here so a quick summary of the main points that we've covered may help.

Data in an OLAP cube is organized into **dimensions** and **measures**:

UnitsSold

Time	Product			
	Sardines	Anchovies	Herrings	Pilchards
April	16	23	12	4
May	14	12	23	6
June	34	19	19	8
July	17	22	14	4

This simple cube has two dimensions – Product and Time. Both have four **members** and there is one **measure** – UnitsSold; so the cube has 16 cells.

The members of a dimension can be (and often are) organized into **hierarchies**; for example, time may be organized into several **levels** such as months, quarters and years. A cell which was the intersection of, say, Sardines and Quarter2 would contain the **aggregated** values for sardines from April, May and June.

We need to extract subsets of data from OLAP cubes and for this we use either **tuples** or **sets**. A tuple is the intersection of one or more members, each of which is taken from a different dimension in a cube. A tuple always identifies a single cell in the multi-dimensional matrix.

A set is a collection of tuples. That collection is usually composed of multiple tuples but can be made up of one or even zero tuples. So, in practice, a set can identify zero, one or more cells in the multi-dimensional matrix.

We sometimes want to store additional data in an OLAP cube but we find that it can't be stored as a measure because it cannot logically be placed at the intersection of all the dimensions. Instead it logically relates to members of a single dimension. For example, the floor area of a store depends simply upon which store we are considering, it doesn't depend upon the month, nor on the product. Such information isn't stored as a measure; it is stored as a **member property** of the appropriate member.

Chapter 2

How MDX is used

MDX is the key to unlocking all of the advanced capabilities of Analysis Services, so once you go beyond building basic cubes and want to add business logic to the cube, you really start to need MDX.

So, is MDX like anything else you are likely to have used? Well, in case you've never seen MDX in the raw, here's a quick example of an MDX query:

```
SELECT
{ [Customers].[All Customers] } ON COLUMNS ,
{ [Measures].[Sales] } ON ROWS
FROM [Sales_MDX1]
WHERE [Time].[1998]
```

The immediately obvious comparison is with SQL. For a start, both languages have names that are TLAs (Three Letter Acronyms) and both are languages designed specifically for querying data structures. They both even use SELECT, FROM and WHERE, which means that the queries you can write with them sound similar.

So MDX is pretty much like SQL? No, despite the apparent similarities, the languages differ in several significant ways.

For a start, SQL isn't simply a query language (despite its name); it also has a whole raft of commands devoted to defining the data structures themselves. In other words you can use all sorts of commands such as CREATE, DROP, INSERT, DELETE etc. to construct and modify your table structures and data. While it is true that you can create local and session OLAP cubes with MDX commands, most general manipulation of the underlying structures is done via the DSO (Decision Support Objects) interface.

On the other hand, MDX can be used for things that SQL can't directly – like defining advanced security settings, custom member roll-ups, custom

29

level roll-ups, actions and so on. (These are all covered during the course of this book.)

Now think about the internal structure of OLAP cubes, as described in Chapter 1 – all those levels, dimensions, hierarchies etc. This is very different from the simple, two-dimensional table structure used by the relational model. SQL doesn't know anything about hierarchies; it doesn't understand the difference between a level and a member, and it knows nothing of a member's properties. MDX does. It knows about all these and more.

The differences go even further. As you are likely to be aware, SQL bends over backwards to take absolutely no notice whatsoever of where a particular row of data happens to be located in a table. You cannot, for example, issue a command in standard SQL which says "Find me the row that relates to Mr. Smith and then return the row beneath that one." SQL will quite happily find you the row that relates to Mr. Smith but it has no concept of where that row is in the table and hence it doesn't know which rows are above or below it.

❛ *There are times when the concept of row position is very useful to solve certain problems, and so some implementations of relational databases provide "cursors" that do allow this sort of positional manipulation. However, cursors aren't part of standard SQL so they immediately, grossly and permanently offend SQL purists.* ❜

MDX on the other hand is built to run against an OLAP cube – an environment where position is all important. The data therein is very sensitive to both structure and position. For example, if I tell you that I am looking at the figures for Q3 2002 and want to compare them with the figures for the previous quarter, you and I intuitively know that the previous quarter is Q2 2002 – there is no sensible alternative. And, impressively, MDX knows it intuitively as well. This is more subtle than it first appears, because it is also level sensitive. If I am looking at the figures for July 2002 then the previous figure is no longer Q2 2002, it is June 2002. MDX is stuffed full of functions that are sensitive to the position of the data, a characteristic which is totally lacking in SQL.

The bottom line is that MDX doesn't really bear much relation to SQL at all, it just happens to look that way when you first see it. That means it's going to be a pain to learn, does it? No, it's fun. In fact, much of the attraction is that it **is** different and we can do so many fun things with it.

So, in broad terms what can we do with MDX?

There are two primary uses of MDX:

- You can use it to write queries: these are full statements with a SELECT, a FROM and a WHERE which, at least superficially, look pretty much like queries written in SQL.
- You can use it to write expressions: snippets of code that can be used for all sorts of purposes such as defining a set, returning one or more values and defining calculated members.

MDX queries

MDX queries are complete stand-alone statements. Many people are already generating MDX queries without even knowing that MDX exists. How? Because the excellent tools that allow you to connect to and query an OLAP cube use a graphical interface which hides the process of writing MDX queries. The user sits at a client machine and looks at the data which can be represented as a bar chart, line graph, pie chart, grid of numbers, whatever. They can use a mouse to slice and dice their way through the data and every time the user makes a selection which requires different data from the cube, the tool generates an MDX query behind the scenes, sends it to the cube, gets an answer back and then displays it for the user. Excel performs this trick when you make use of its pivoting abilities to inspect data in a cube, and the same is true of tools like ProClarity.

MDX expressions

MDX expressions, on the other hand, are partial statements. They're small but highly useful chunks of code that are used for all sorts of purposes. For example, they can be used to create calculated members which add significant power to analysis cubes, as we'll see later.

This book introduces both MDX queries and MDX expressions but we'll spend much more time on the expressions than on the queries. Again, if you approach MDX from a SQL perspective, this seems weird because querying is so important in SQL. However, in MDX this isn't the case. In addition, as we have said, there are some very good MDX querying tools around which you can use to generate the MDX for you.

For example, this is ProClarity's highly graphical user interface:

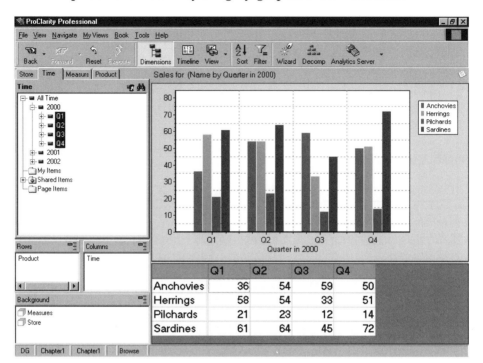

You can use the graphical interface to drill up and down through the data – ProClarity takes care of generating the required MDX behind the scenes. One outstanding feature is that ProClarity allows you, at any time, to view the MDX it has generated and edit it (if you so desire) using the MDX Editor that is built in to the product.

So tools like ProClarity are not only great tool for end users, they are also very handy for teaching developers about MDX queries. If you aren't sure what syntax to use, design the query using the GUI and then sneak a look at the MDX.

🖢 *The MDX code generated by these tools is always syntactically correct and works fine. Like most algorithmically written code it can, on occasions, be a little verbose. However, it always shows you the correct overall form of the query and you can always hone your skills by hand-tuning it to a neater and more concise form. For example the code above can be simplified to:* 🖢

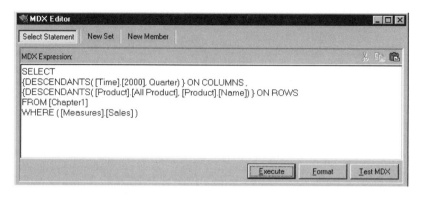

One other facet of software generated MDX is that it often includes ampersands (&). When you are starting to use MDX you can safely ignore these. At the end of Chapter 14 we have a section that explains why they are there, but we recommend that you leave it until then because the explanation only makes sense when you have gained some experience with the language.

🖢 *However, if we have piqued your curiosity, please feel free to read it now.* 🖢

So, given that you have a tool like ProClarity or Excel around, you never need to hand-write MDX queries yourself. MDX expressions, on the other hand, are used much more widely. They are used to add business logic to the cubes, to define security, color coding, exception alerting – in other words, almost everywhere. Unless you are building very simple OLAP databases, the chances are that you will want to use MDX expressions somewhere. With all of this in mind we have concentrated mainly on MDX expressions.

However, this book would be woefully incomplete without **some** information about querying, so we'll start by looking at MDX queries in the next chapter and use them to introduce the basic syntax of MDX. From then on we'll concentrate mainly on MDX expressions, but to finish off (in Chapter 18) we'll return to queries to fill in a little more detail.

Chapter 3

MDX queries

This chapter is an introduction to using MDX to query OLAP cubes and we're also using it to introduce you to MDX syntax in general.

Since we're starting on the practical work, you may want to try the MDX statements for yourself. The cube we're using is available in the CAB file called FoodMart2000_MDX1.CAB and restores as a database called FoodMart2000_MDX1. It is based on the standard FoodMart database that is supplied as part of Analysis Services. In turn, that database contains two cubes – we'll be using the one called Sales_MDX1. We've put all of the MDX statements used in this chapter in a text file called CHAP3.TXT so that you can cut and paste them into whatever front-end tool you want to use to send queries to the cube. See Appendix 1 for information about where these files are located and how you can use them. If you want to use the copy of ProClarity as your front-end tool, see Appendix 2 for instructions on how to install it and about how to use its built-in MDX editor.

In fact, we're going to be using the FoodMart2000_MDX1 database for chapters 3 to 7 inclusive. In some of those chapters we make significant changes to the cubes in the database. We thoroughly recommend that you follow along with the examples and modify the cubes for yourself. However, in case you have any difficulties, we have also included a CAB file called FoodMart2000_EndChap7 which, as you might guess, has all of the work from those five chapters completed for you.

Resources:

    Starting database – FoodMart2000_MDX1
    Cube – Sales_MDX1
    Completed sample database – FoodMart2000_EndChap7
    MDX samples – CHAP3.TXT

Using MDX for queries

MDX queries can't be used in isolation; in other words, you can't just squirt one to an OLAP cube from thin air, you have to send it from some sort of front-end application. If you are a hardcore programmer, you will probably want to write the front-end for yourself in assembler; those people who actually have lives tend to use something like Excel, ProClarity, Business Objects etc.

Whatever front-end you use, it is going to be receiving an answer back from the cube. MDX queries return data from one or more cells. Using an MDX query you can ask for (and get back from the cube) an array of data with anything up to 128 dimensions. *(Yes, we are using the word 'array' here in a desperate attempt to avoid using the word 'set' because, as discussed in the earlier chapters, the word 'set' has a very specific meaning in MDX. Essentially a query returns the values from a collection of cells that form part of the original OLAP cube.)* Users can elect to see the data that comes back in a whole variety of ways (pie chart, bar graph, grid etc.).

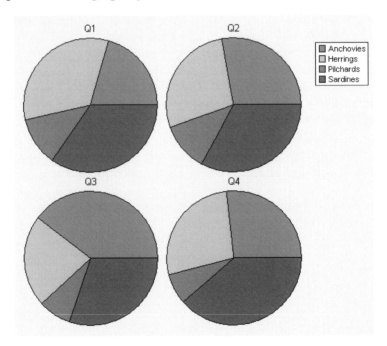

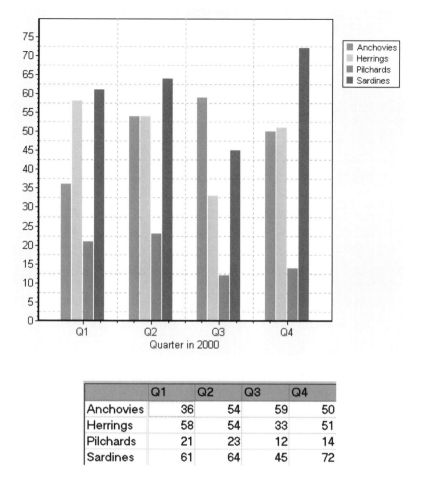

	Q1	Q2	Q3	Q4
Anchovies	36	54	59	50
Herrings	58	54	33	51
Pilchards	21	23	12	14
Sardines	61	64	45	72

However, this choice is made using the front-end tool and is not specified in the MDX query that is sent to the OLAP cube. If, in this chapter, we mainly think of the data coming back as the grids of data rather than as charts, it will make it easier to understand how the MDX is working.

The cube we're using has the structure shown overleaf.

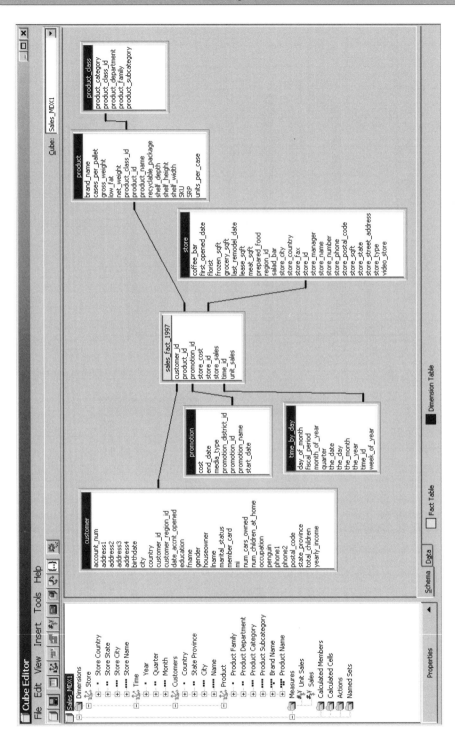

The tree pane on the left shows us that there are four dimensions by which the user can slice and dice the data – Store, Time, Customers and Product. (Not all of the dimension tables shown in the Schema Tab on the right are used in this cube.) The cube also has two measures – Unit Sales and Sales.

MDX has to be able to specify not only where the data comes from in the cube, but also how it is going to be structured in the grid that is sent to the front-end application.

Data extracted from an OLAP cube can be defined in terms of sets and tuples; the grids of data that appear in the front-end tool can be defined in terms of columns and rows.

Imagine that you want to produce the simplest possible two-dimensional grid – just a set of rows and columns; something like:

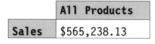

	All Products
Sales	$565,238.13

❢ *In this case we've even reduced it down to one row and one column, but we'll expand it in a minute.* ❢

The components that an MDX query needs in order to extract the requested information from the OLAP cube and display it like this are:

- a component to specify the column headers
- a component to specify the row headers
- a pointer to the cube we are using

The first two components are going to be sets (as described in Chapter 1); the third is simply going to be the name of the cube.

SELECT, FROM, ON COLUMNS, ON ROWS

MDX spells this out as follows:

```
SELECT
{set defining the column headers} ON COLUMNS,
{set defining the row headers} ON ROWS
FROM [cube name]
```

An example of a working MDX query looks like this:

```
SELECT
{[Product].[All Products]} ON COLUMNS,
{[Measures].[Sales]} ON ROWS
FROM [Sales_MDX1]
```

❦ *Assuming that you have read Chapter 1, you are probably looking at* {[Product].[All Products]} *trying to work out if it really is a set, or whether we have got it wrong and it is a tuple. The answer is that it is a set. As we said in Chapter 1, a set is composed of a collection of tuples, including a collection that simply has one tuple in it. In this first example of a query we are keeping the data as simple as possible, so we are using a set that is composed of a single tuple. We'll make it more complicated in a minute.*

Oh, and ignore the brackets briefly; we'll explain their usage in Chapter 4 after you have got the overall plan. ❦

If you now hand-write this statement into a front-end tool like ProClarity (or cut and paste it from the text file), as long as that tool is connected to the correct cube, it will produce output something like this:

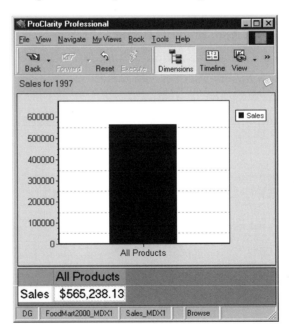

Note, incidentally, that this screen shot shows the Sales for 1997. This cube has four dimensions and our MDX statement has only specified one of them here – namely Product. Since it doesn't specify anything about the other three, Analysis Services assumes that we want to take data from the default member. This is usually the highest level of each un-named dimension – which is typically the All level. However, in this particular cube, there is no All level in the Time dimension – as this screen shot from Analysis Services shows when we examine the data using the data tab.

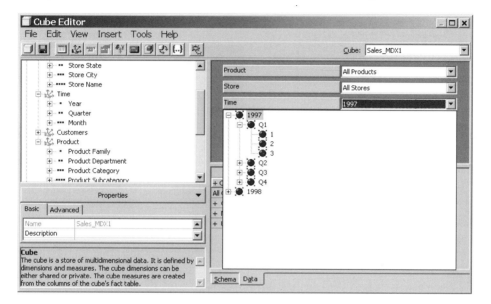

And the same can be seen from ProClarity.

In the case where a dimension isn't specified and there isn't an All level, Analysis Services will, by default, use the first member from the highest level. In our Time dimension this is 1997.

❝ *Let's summarize default members. You can set the default member of a dimension using its **Default Member** property in Analysis Manager. If you don't explicitly specify one, the default member is the All member. Of course, you are not obliged to have an All member, in which case Analysis Services will choose a member from the highest level.* ❞

OK, that was easy. What if we want to reverse the rows and columns? We simply swap over the sets like this:

```
SELECT
{[Measures].[Sales]} ON COLUMNS,
{[Product].[All Products]} ON ROWS
FROM [Sales_MDX1]
```

The answer is the same and so is the bar chart.

Now, suppose that we want to see a little more detail, and we happen to know that the products can be broken down into three product families – food, drink and non-consumables. We can simply alter the set that is pointing to all products and get it to point to the members of the next level down, like this:

```
SELECT
{[Measures].[Sales]} ON COLUMNS,
{[Product].[All Products].[Food],
[Product].[All Products].[Drink],
[Product].[All Products].[Non-Consumable]} ON ROWS
FROM [Sales_MDX1]
```

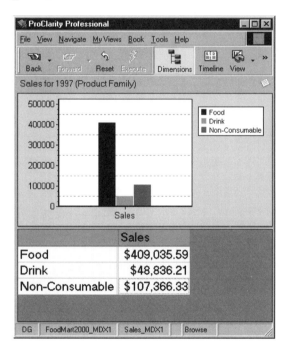

Just to emphasise the point that we made earlier (about the fact that the interface depiction of the data is independent of the MDX statement that retrieves the data) you can use the interface options in your front-end tool:

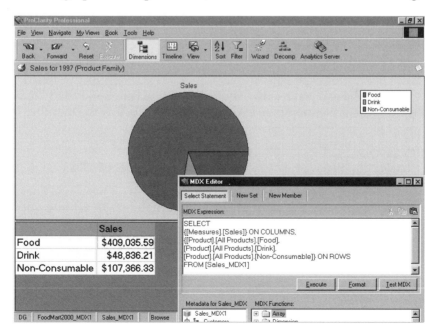

to alter the graph that is produced, while the MDX remains unchanged.

Excellent! Now we also happen to know that there are fifteen members underneath the member Food, so in order to show them we can write an MDX statement that lists all fifteen:

```
SELECT
{[Measures].[Sales]} ON COLUMNS,
{[Product].[Product Family].[Food].[Baked Goods],
[Product].[Product Family].[Food].[Baking Goods],
[Product].[Product Family].[Food].[Breakfast Foods],
[Product].[Product Family].[Food].[Canned Foods],
[Product].[Product Family].[Food].[Canned Products],
[Product].[Product Family].[Food].[Dairy],
[Product].[Product Family].[Food].[Deli],
[Product].[Product Family].[Food].[Eggs],
[Product].[Product Family].[Food].[Frozen Foods],
[Product].[Product Family].[Food].[Meat],
[Product].[Product Family].[Food].[Produce],
[Product].[Product Family].[Food].[Seafood],
[Product].[Product Family].[Food].[Snack Foods],
[Product].[Product Family].[Food].[Snacks],
[Product].[Product Family].[Food].[Starchy Foods]} ON ROWS
FROM [Sales_MDX1]
```

At this point you could be forgiven for thinking "Just a minute! Are you mad? You really expect me to type all of this into an editor and get it right?"

No, we're just kidding (although this MDX query does run and does produce the correct answer). We said in Chapter 1 that MDX is a language specifically built for querying OLAP cubes, so it has a whole host of functions that are designed to make this sort of task easier.

For example, we can replace the above list with a function called Children that returns all of the members in the level directly below the member Food:

```
SELECT
{[Measures].[Sales]} ON COLUMNS,
{[Product].[Product Family].[Food].Children} ON ROWS
FROM [Sales_MDX1]
```

which returns exactly the same answer... but manages to ask the question rather more succinctly.

6 *Incidentally, you'll notice that these last two queries are using one of the alternative naming conventions (`dimension.level.name`) to point to the members, as discussed in Chapter 1. The more common naming convention (`dimension.name.name`), of course, works equally well:*

```
SELECT
{[Measures].[Sales]} ON COLUMNS,
{[Product].[All Products].[Food].Children} ON ROWS
FROM [Sales_MDX1]
```

and, in fact, this is the form of the query that we have provided in the text file. **9**

Hopefully, you are now really interested in functions like `Children` because they are clearly mind-bogglingly useful in MDX. There's more about them in Chapter 6.

Suppose that you want to use two dimensions to slice and dice the Unit Sales measure to produce a grid like this:

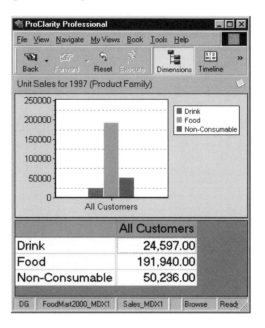

Have a go at working out the MDX required. If this is your first introduction to MDX, this may be a tough one, but it is worth persevering. You are now specifying two of the dimensions – Customers and Product. You need All Customers on the columns and the children of All Products on the rows. You also need to know that if no measures member is specified, then Analysis Services will use the default measure, or, if none is set, its own arbitrary choice (usually the first one in the list). In this case that happens to be what we want, Unit Sales, so you can forget about that for the moment.

One answer (there are others) is:

```
SELECT
{[Customers].[All Customers]} ON COLUMNS,
{[Product].[All Products].Children} ON ROWS
FROM [Sales_MDX1]
```

OK, now try this one. We want to expand this to show Unit Sales for the same product groups but we want to drill down into the customer dimension as far as the three US states represented in this data (California, Oregon and Washington).

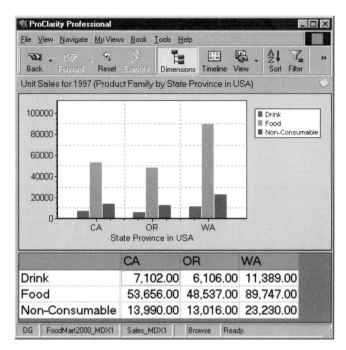

We're working on a need-to-know basis... and what you need to know here is that these three states are the children of [Customers].[All Customers].[USA] in the customer hierarchy.

So the obvious answer is simply to modify the above statement to:

```
SELECT
{[Customers].[All Customers].[USA].Children} ON COLUMNS ,
{[Product].[All Products].Children} ON ROWS
FROM [Sales_MDX1]
```

WHERE

This works fine, and all is well in MDX land. But suppose you don't want to use the Unit Sales measure; instead you want to use Sales. No problem, you can use the WHERE clause to give you precisely this control.

```
SELECT
{[Customers].[All Customers].[USA].Children} ON COLUMNS,
{[Product].[All Products].Children} ON ROWS
FROM [Sales_MDX1]
WHERE ([Measures].[Sales])
```

This produces:

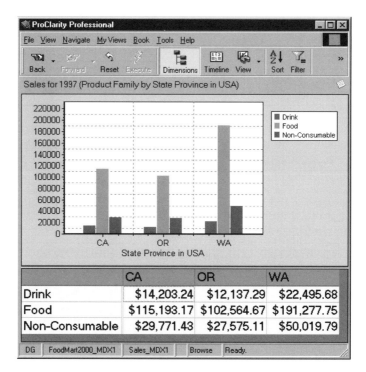

	CA	OR	WA
Drink	$14,203.24	$12,137.29	$22,495.68
Food	$115,193.17	$102,564.67	$191,277.75
Non-Consumable	$29,771.43	$27,575.11	$50,019.79

The WHERE clause works pretty much as you would expect. In this case it says "show me this data where the measure involved is Sales". However, the WHERE clause certainly isn't restricted to measures, nor is it restricted to a single dimension. For example, the following is a perfectly legal MDX query:

```
SELECT
{[Customers].[All Customers].[USA].Children} ON COLUMNS ,
{[Product].[All Products].Children} ON ROWS
FROM [Sales_MDX1]
WHERE ([Measures].[Sales], [Time].[1998])
```

and will show you exactly the same output as above, except for the year 1998.

And:

```
SELECT
{[Customers].[All Customers].[USA].Children} ON COLUMNS ,
{[Product].[All Products].Children} ON ROWS
FROM [Sales_MDX1]
WHERE ([Measures].[Sales], [Time].[1998].[Q1])
```

essentially says "Show me the Sales for the first quarter of 1998 for each US state and product group." And that is exactly what you get.

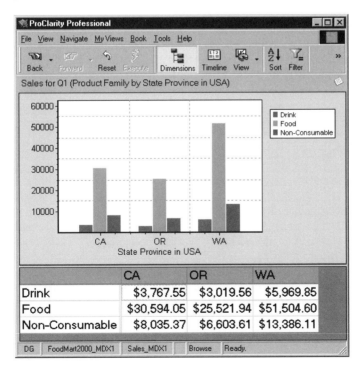

	CA	OR	WA
Drink	$3,767.55	$3,019.56	$5,969.85
Food	$30,594.05	$25,521.94	$51,504.60
Non-Consumable	$8,035.37	$6,603.61	$13,386.11

Slicer

More formally, we can refer to whatever is in the WHERE clause as the slicer. So the above MDX query could also be described as saying "show me the US customers and product groups for the measures = sales, time.1998.Q1 slice." Or, indeed, "show me the US customers and product groups sliced by sales and Q1 1998."

It is also worth knowing that any dimensions not explicitly referenced in the MDX query are assumed to be slicer dimensions and, as such, will filter the data with their default members (see above).

Summary

MDX queries are very powerful and relatively simple to write; we've used them in this chapter to introduce you to the general MDX syntax. We suspect that you will often, in practice, use a front-end tool to generate queries for you; however, just in case you are interested in understanding how more complex queries can be written, we've put some more detail in Chapter 18.

In the rest of the book we are going to be mostly using expressions to illustrate more complex aspects of MDX, but always bear in mind that most of the information that you learn about expressions can be applied equally to MDX queries.

Chapter 4

MDX syntax

Resources:

Starting database – FoodMart2000_MDX1
Cube – Sales_MDX1
Completed sample database – FoodMart2000_EndChap7
MDX samples – CHAP4.TXT

Brackets, braces and the odd dot and comma

Now that you've seen how MDX works in practice, this seems like a good time to explain the use of brackets and braces.

Brackets [ ] – Dimension names and member names

Firstly, there are brackets [ ] which are called 'square brackets' in UK parlance. Dimension names and member names are enclosed within brackets. You can enclose all such names in brackets, though it is only syntactically obligatory if the name contains numbers, spaces, other special characters or is a keyword. For example, From is a keyword, and if there is dimension called From, it should be encoded as [From]. When the MDX parser comes across, for example, a number, it expects to be able treat it as a number; the brackets tell it that it's a name that just happens to contain numerical information.

Here are six syntactically correct dimension or member names:

```
[All Products]
Drink
[Penguin]
[Q3]
[Drink]
Penguin
```

In the real world you are likely to see MDX written with a mix of bracketed and unbracketed names. Code generation tools (like ProClarity) tend always to put brackets in because it's easier to write an algorithm that always puts them in than to write one that determines whether brackets are syntactically necessary or not. Humans, on the other hand, like short cuts and are more likely to use brackets only when necessary; however, they often use a GUI tool to do the grunt work and then hand-tweak the code – the result is the mix you often find.

❝ *During the course of planning and writing the book, we've swung to opposite ends of the spectrum (should we always use brackets? should we use them only when obligatory?) and ended up feeling that our examples ought to represent real code. You'll find that our examples run true to the real world description above and mix bracketing and non-bracketing with impunity. Our hand-typed code tends to be low on brackets while the code we've cut and pasted from ProClarity's MDX editor is full of the things. Apologies are proffered in advance to anyone who is offended.* ❞

Dots . – Separators

When you use a dimension name and several member names together in order to drill down into a hierarchy to find a particular member, you need to separate the names with dots, like this:

```
[Product].[Drink].[Beverages]
```

Braces ( ) – Tuples

Braces ( ) – brackets in UK English – are used to denote tuples, a tuple is (as detailed in Chapter 1) a collection of members, each taken from a different dimension that points to some data in which we're interested. More precisely, a tuple is the intersection of one or more members, each of which is taken from a different dimension in a cube.

Tuples, you'll recall, are defined in terms of dimensions and members which, as you now know, may themselves have to be wrapped in brackets.

So, a simple tuple would be syntactically represented as:

```
([Product].[Drink].[Beverages])
```

Tuples can, and usually do, contain references to several members. A comma is required to separate each member in the tuple. Here are tuples with two and three members respectively, separated by commas and inside braces:

```
([Product].[Drink].[Beverages], [Customers].[USA])
```

```
([Product].[Drink].[Beverages], [Customers].[USA],
[Time].[1998])
```

Curly braces { } – Sets

And now for curly braces { }, or curly brackets, depending on your location in the world. These are used to denote sets. As detailed in Chapter 1, a set is a collection of tuples with the same dimensionality.

So the following are perfectly respectable examples of sets:

```
{([Product].[Drink].[Beverages]),
([Product].[Food].[Produce])}
```

```
{[Customers].[All Customers].[USA].Children}
```

```
{[Product].[All Products].Children}
```

```
{[Product].[Product Family].[Food].[Baked Goods],
[Product].[Product Family].[Food].[Baking Goods],
[Product].[Product Family].[Food].[Breakfast Foods],
[Product].[Product Family].[Food].[Canned Foods]}
```

You remember that we said earlier that a set may be composed of more than one tuple, but it can also comprise only one tuple, or even zero tuples, in which case it is an empty set. Well, we can illustrate this by going briefly back to the SELECT statement that we covered in Chapter 3.

The SELECT statement is expecting you to specify sets for the columns and rows. In addition, if we are inquisitive, we can test this by trying to send an MDX query to Analysis Services with tuples instead of sets. Something like this will do:

```
SELECT
([Measures].[Sales]) ON COLUMNS,
{[Product].[All Products].Children} ON ROWS
FROM [Sales_MDX1]
```

We are using a tuple for the ON COLUMNS statement and a set for the ON ROWS. The result is an error message to the effect that the member cannot be converted to a set.

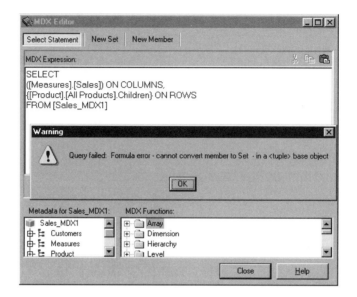

OK, what happens if we explicitly tell Analysis Services that this is a set and not a tuple? All we have to do is to wrap up the tuple in curly braces like this:

```
SELECT
{([Measures].[Sales])} ON COLUMNS,
{[Product].[All Products].Children} ON ROWS
FROM [Sales_MDX1]
```

This ensures that the query runs fine. We've told Analysis Services that this is a set and a set can be a single tuple, so Analysis Services is happy and will run the query.

In fact, we can, in this case, dispense with the braces that distinguish the contents of the set as a tuple, like this:

```
SELECT
{[Measures].[Sales]} ON COLUMNS,
{[Product].[All Products].Children} ON ROWS
FROM [Sales_MDX1]
```

and the query runs serenely as before because this is now a set, not a tuple. It just happens to be a set that comprises of a single tuple.

If it sounds like we are laboring this point it is simply that we have found that, when teaching people to use MDX, they often get bogged down here. So a useful and really simple trick is, when your MDX statements are failing to work, try wrapping up your tuples in curly braces. If the MDX statement you are using was expecting a set, this should cure the problem.

Chapter 5

MDX expressions

Resources:

Starting database – `FoodMart2000_MDX1`
Cube – `Sales_MDX1`
Completed sample database – `FoodMart2000_EndChap7`
MDX samples – `CHAP5.TXT`

In Chapter 2 we said that MDX is typically used for querying OLAP cubes and also for expressions, so here we'll start looking at creating and using MDX expressions. Expressions may take a tuple or set as a parameter and **always** return a value (even if it is a null); MDX doesn't have any notion of 'void'. Expressions are partial MDX statements and they have a host of uses such as defining calculated members, sets, or member properties.

Calculated members are one of the more common ways in which MDX expressions are put to work and they can be created for any dimension. This includes the measures dimension; indeed calculated measures are the most common type of calculated member.

Calculated measures enable you to use existing information in a cube to generate further information that can tell you more about your business. For instance, you can calculate the growth or slump in sales figures. You can calculate this as currency amounts or as percentages and you can work out factors such as the average sales over specific periods. Data generated with calculated members makes it easier to see exceptions to the expected behavior of your business, enhancing the probability of spotting peaks and troughs in performance. Such information gives you the opportunity to react more quickly to unexpected changes.

Operationally, calculated measures are computed at runtime so there is no processing penalty for you either in terms of the time it takes to process your cube or in the number of aggregations that have to be stored. The only hit you take is at runtime, when the cube is queried and in practice the calculations are very, very fast so the overall hit is negligible in most cases.

We'll start the practical work below and write some simple MDX expressions which we'll use in calculated members, but first just a very brief recap of cell naming.

Recap of cell naming

In a spreadsheet like Excel, every cell has a co-ordinate/name that is unique to that cell, for example, B7 or C8. The same idea is true of OLAP cubes. Every cell is a tuple (see Chapter 1) and every tuple has a unique name so each cell, by definition, has a unique name.

We can illustrate this with a simple, three-dimensional cube:

- Products which contains Clothing, Appliances and Groceries
- Time, which contains the years 1997 through 2001
- Measures which contains Sales, Costs and Units.

❦ *Note that, as discussed in Chapter 1, we are essentially treating Measures as just another dimension. Note also that this is simply a theoretical cube in order to keep the MDX simple – it isn't one of our sample cubes.* ❦

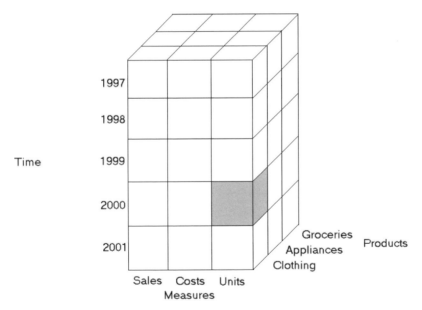

Now, consider the cell highlighted here. We can reference the appropriate member in Products by saying:

```
Products.Clothing
```

We can see that the cell is in the year 2000 so we can say:

```
Time.[2000]
```

and the cell clearly refers to the Units measure:

```
Measures.Units
```

So the correct way to reference this cell, that is, the tuple that refers to this cell is:

```
(Products.Clothing, Measures.Units, Time.[2000])
```

We can do the same for another cell, just to make the point that all of them have unique names.

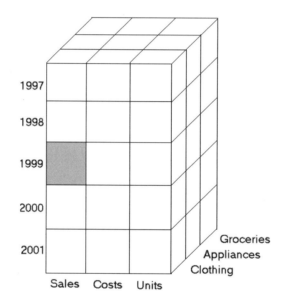

```
(Products.Clothing, Measures.Sales, Time.[1999])
```

The concept of the current cell

OK, so each cell has a unique name – a tuple. But what happens when we want to write an MDX expression that refers not to a specific cell in the cube, but to the one in which we are currently interested? Easy, we can reference the 'current cell' by using a function called CurrentMember.

Basically, what CurrentMember says is "you are here", rather like the well-fingered arrow on a map displayed in a public place. It's a little smarter than that, however, in the sense that it is a dynamic "you are here". As you (or the user of your cube) move around, the CurrentMember moves around with you.

So another way to refer to the cell:

```
(Products.Clothing, Measures.Units, Time.[2000])
```

would be to say:

```
(Products.CurrentMember, Measures.CurrentMember,
Time.CurrentMember)
```

This is a completely generic way to refer to any co-ordinate across those three dimensions.

❧ *At this point you may be thinking "OK, so we now have a name that seems to be able to point to any cell in the cube. What use is that?" It does get to be useful, honest; and before the end of the chapter as well.* ❧

Relative cell referencing

Let's go back to our diagram for a moment:

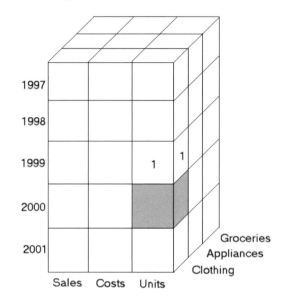

The highlighted cell is:

```
(Products.Clothing, Measures.Units, Time.[2000])
```

and let's assume for a minute that it is also the current cell, so it can also be referenced as:

```
(Products.CurrentMember, Measures.CurrentMember,
Time.CurrentMember)
```

How can we reference the cell above it, the one which has been labeled with a "1"?

Well, it can, perfectly accurately, be referred to as:

```
(Products.Clothing, Measures.Units, Time.[1999])
```

However, the only difference between the gray cell and the one labeled "1" is in the Time dimension. Conveniently there is an MDX function called PrevMember which you can use on any of the dimensions (including Time) so this new cell can also be referenced as:

```
(Products.Clothing, Measures.Units, Time.[2000].PrevMember)
```

`Time.[2000]` was the known entity so we go back one member by using the PrevMember function (the name is taken from, as you might guess, "Previous Member" but you have to use the contraction PrevMember).

OK, suppose that we want to refer to a cell which is one ahead in Time; that is, to the cell labeled "2" below?

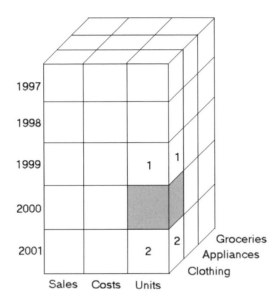

There is another MDX function, very similar to PrevMember, called NextMember. So "2" can be referenced as:

`(Products.Clothing, Measures.Units, Time.[2000].NextMember)`

In Chapter 2 we said that MDX differs from SQL because it is sensitive to the position of the data within the data structure; here you can see this 'awareness' of position working in practice.

Now a more challenging example: what about a cell that is several members removed? It's labeled with a "3" below.

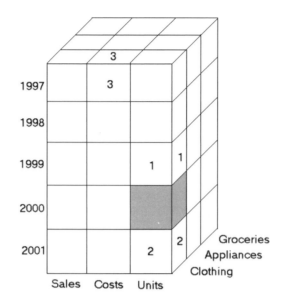

You see that the cell in question is back one member from Units and back three members from 2000. You know about PrevMember – so can you say this?

    PrevMember.PrevMember.PrevMember

Well, the answer is that you can. You could use multiple PrevMember to go back several steps, but it's not at all elegant. You get long, long expressions that are difficult to understand and error-prone to write. So there is an MDX function called Lag designed especially for this case. To go back three levels on the Time dimension we say:

    Time.[2000].Lag(3)

So we can refer to the cell as:

    (Products.Clothing, Measures.Units.PrevMember,
    Time.[2000].Lag(3))

What if you wanted to refer to a cell not three periods back but two ahead? There's another function that's similar and a parallel to Lag(), called Lead(), so we'd use Lead(2). In fact, just to make life simpler (or more complex, depending upon your point of view) both Lag and Lead can take negative parameters, so you **could** use the Lead function to refer to cell "3" as:

```
(Products.Clothing, Measures.Units.PrevMember,
Time.[2000].Lead(-3))
```

❦ *So if you're a pessimistic person you can always use Lag, even to move forward. If you're an optimist you can ignore the Lag function, use Lead all the time and put a negative parameter in whenever necessary.* ❧

That background information is enough to allow us to start using calculated measures in earnest and to make this as useful as possible, we'll illustrate their use by solving three common business problems. The cube we'll be working with is Sales_MDX1, which is the same one we used in Chapter 3 and we'll be using it for the next chapter as well. In this cube there are Measures for Sales (in dollars) and Unit Sales.

The practicalities – how to look at the data in a cube

We'll start with a brief introduction to using the tools in Analysis Manager to look at data in a cube (rather than using a front-end tool as we did in Chapter 3), then we'll introduce our first business problem and solve it by creating a calculated member. This and the following two problems all come under the general heading of time-series analysis.

With Analysis Manager installed and the cubes from the CD-ROM restored, navigate down the Tree view on the left, expand the FoodMart2000_MDX1 database and the Cubes folder. You should see a cube called Sales_MDX1. Right click upon it and select Browse Data from the menu that pops out. This opens the Cube Browser.

Cube Browser - Sales_MDX1			_ □ ×
Product		All Products	▼
Store		All Stores	▼
Time		1997	▼

	MeasuresLevel	
+ Country	Unit Sales	Sales
All Customers	266,773.00	$565,238.13
+ Canada		
+ Mexico		
+ USA	266,773.00	$565,238.13

Double-click a member to drill up or down.   [Close]   Help

The top section shows the Product, Store and Time dimensions as raised buttons and in the pane below there is a grid which shows data from the Customers dimension and from the two measures.

You can drill down into the data in the grid by clicking on any label that is preceded by a plus symbol: double clicking on USA, for instance, expands to show three states and doing it again collapses the states back into their country. Any label preceded by a minus symbol can be collapsed.

Click and drag the raised button that indicates the Time dimension in the area above the grid, releasing the mouse button when it's right over the button labeled '+ Country' on the grid. (The mouse pointer will change to an icon looking like a four-paned window with a diagonal double-headed arrow in the top right pane). The contents of the grid will change to showing the two measures in relation to the Time dimension, and the Customers dimension will be popped back into the area above the grid.

Cube Browser - Sales_MDX1		_ □ ×
Product	All Products	▼
Store	All Stores	▼
Customers	All Customers	▼

	MeasuresLevel	
+ Year	Unit Sales	Sales
+ 1997	266,773.00	$565,238.13
+ 1998	509,987.00	$1,079,147.47

Double-click a member to drill up or down.　　Close　　Help

Now you can click to drill down through the levels of the Time hierarchy. You can add further dimensions by clicking and dragging: here both the Time and Customers dimensions are shown.

Cube Browser - Sales_MDX1

| Product | All Products |
| Store | All Stores |

		MeasuresLevel	
+ Year	+ Country	Unit Sales	Sales
	All Customers	266,773.00	$565,238.13
+ 1997	+ Canada		
	+ Mexico		
	+ USA	266,773.00	$565,238.13
	All Customers	509,987.00	$1,079,147.47
+ 1998	+ Canada	46,157.00	$98,045.46
	+ Mexico	203,914.00	$430,293.59
	+ USA	259,916.00	$550,808.42

Double-click a member to drill up or down.　　　　Close　　Help

There is another way to inspect data, and it's worth using when you're learning (we use it for many of our screen shots) because it shows a bit more about the structure of the data. Close the Cube Browser, right click on the cube again and this time, select Edit.... This opens the Cube Editor.

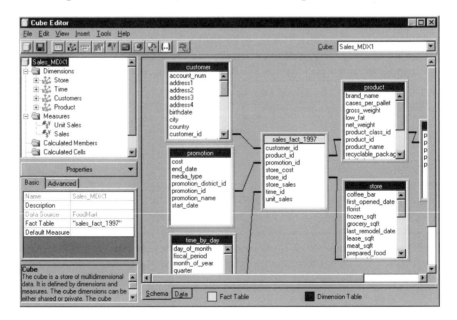

There is a tree pane for navigation at the top left and below that the properties of the selected item are shown with brief descriptive text beneath. The tree pane shows that the cube has four dimensions – Store, Time, Customers and Product – and two measures – Unit Sales and Sales. The name of the cube is shown in the top right and the rest of the right side of the screen is given up to the schema view of the cube. The tables from which the cube is built are displayed: one fact table with many dimension tables strung from it.

There are two tabs below the schema view, labeled Schema (currently on view) and Data: click the Data tab. The left side of the screen remains unchanged and the right side gives you the same view as the Cube Browser and is driven as described above.

1 Comparing values

We'll start with a very simple collection of data rather than the data from the cube, just to illustrate how this works.

❦ *We would normally say "set of data" but given that the word 'set' has a specific meaning in MDX, the word 'collection' seems safer.* ❧

Year	Quarter	Month	Sales
2000			790
	Q1		120
		January	30
		February	40
		March	50
	Q2		200
		April	65
		May	45
		June	90
	Q3		185
		July	55
		August	60
		September	70
	Q4		285
		October	80
		November	100
		December	105

You can see that the measure is Sales and that the Time dimension has three levels: Year, Quarter and Month. Suppose we focus our attention on a particular member at a particular level (say, February at the Month level) and want to know how sales have improved since the previous month (January). Can we write an MDX statement to do that? Yes, we could write one that does exactly and precisely that (and nothing else) but we can also do better. Using what we have just learnt about CurrentMember and PrevMember, we can write an expression that's going to work for all members of the Month level. Better still, it will work for all members at all levels in the Time dimension.

What we have to do is to create a calculated member with this expression:

```
(Time.CurrentMember, Measures.Sales) —
(Time.CurrentMember.PrevMember, Measures.Sales)
```

This calculated measure (a calculated member in the Measures dimension) derives a whole new value that we didn't know beforehand. The first part of the expression identifies the cell we're interested in (the sales for February) and subtracts from it the sales figure for January which is identified by the second part of the expression. The value the expression returns is 10, the difference between 40 and 30. How this works is best summed up with a diagram.

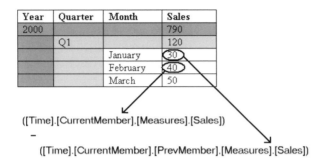

Year	Quarter	Month	Sales
2000			790
	Q1		120
		January	30
		February	40
		March	50

([Time].[CurrentMember].[Measures].[Sales])

–

([Time].[CurrentMember].[PrevMember].[Measures].[Sales])

The beauty of this expression is that Time.CurrentMember is level sensitive, so if we swap to a different level:

Year	Quarter	Month	Sales
2000			790
	Q1		120
		January	30
		February	40
		March	50
	Q2		200
		April	65
		May	45
		June	90

([Time].[CurrentMember].[Measures].[Sales])

–

([Time].[CurrentMember].[PrevMember].[Measures].[Sales])

it still works. So if the CurrentMember is a month, then the PrevMember is the previous month. If CurrentMember is a quarter, then PrevMember is the previous quarter, which is just how it should be.

OK, that's the theory; now let's do some practical stuff and build a calculated member using the Sales_MDX1 cube.

The practicalities – how to create a calculated member

In the tree view of the Cube Editor you'll see a folder called Calculated Members which is empty at present. Right click upon it and select the New Calculated Member... option that appears. This opens the Calculated Member Builder:

The Parent dimension is already in place: as we said above, mostly we'll be creating calculated measures and so Measures is quite correct here.

Type in a Member name: Sales Growth is good. The Value expression is where we put the MDX code that defines the calculation: this is what we thrashed out above:

```
(Time.CurrentMember, Measures.Sales) –
(Time.CurrentMember.PrevMember, Measures.Sales)
```

❡ *MDX can be typed in and/or cut and pasted in from a text editor or word processor. All of these expressions are in a text file called CHAP5.TXT on the CD-ROM. You can also build up an expression by selecting objects from the Data and Functions panes. On the left, the Data pane shows the cube structure (dimensions and levels) and in the middle, the Functions pane shows a list of all the MDX functions. When you highlight a function, its syntax is shown at the bottom of the screen. Also, the Calculated Member Builder automatically uses color to highlight various parts of an expression. Functions are shown in red, for instance, and some bracket matching is performed so if you have an orphan bracket, it will be highlighted in red to draw your attention to it.*

Click the Check box to test the syntax and all being well, you should see this:

Now click the OK button and inspect the new measure from the Cube Editor:

		MeasuresLevel	
- Quarter	Month	Sales	Sales Growth
1997 Total		$565,238.13	$565,238.13
	Q1 Total	$139,628.35	$139,628.35
- Q1	1	$45,539.69	$45,539.69
	2	$44,058.79	-$1,480.90
	3	$50,029.87	$5,971.08
+ Q2	Q2 Total	$132,666.27	-$6,962.08
+ Q3	Q3 Total	$140,271.89	$7,605.62
+ Q4	Q4 Total	$152,671.62	$12,399.73
1998 Total		$1,079,147.47	$513,909.34
	Q1 Total	$290,873.18	$138,201.56
- Q1	1	$98,155.28	$41,189.64
	2	$94,498.00	-$3,657.28
	3	$98,219.90	$3,721.90
	Q2 Total	$287,009.99	-$3,863.19
- Q2	4	$94,776.14	-$3,443.76
	5	$95,183.81	$407.67
	6	$97,050.04	$1,866.23
+ Q3	Q3 Total	$295,040.55	$8,030.56
+ Q4	Q4 Total	$206,223.75	-$88,816.80

and there are the newly generated figures.

❧ *We've expanded Time so that we can see some of the detail for Quarter and Month and we have trimmed the screen so that it is more readable on the page.*

The sales growth for Month 2 in 1998, for instance, is an uninspiring –$3,657.28. This and the other negative numbers have already given us a greater understanding of our fictitious company. The good news is that this is just a first simple example of what can be done with calculated members; there's much more to come.

> *Incidentally, if you decide to look at a calculated member from a front-end tool like ProClarity, make sure that you first save the new measure in the Cube Editor and then refresh the view from ProClarity by selecting File, Open Cube.*

It's worth noting that the `CurrentMember` is always the default, so the expression above could be condensed a little to:

```
(Time.CurrentMember, Measures.Sales) -
(Time.PrevMember, Measures.Sales)
```

It will be understood that you're referring to the previous member from the current member and it saves you a little bit of typing.

> *During the proof-reading stage Mosha, who really does know about this sort of thing in detail, added:*
>
> *"Saying that 'CurrentMember is always the default' is a little vague. CurrentMember is a default property of the dimension. Therefore, the expression can be simplified even further to:*

```
([Time], Sales) - ([Time].PrevMember, Sales)
```

> *or even to*

```
Sales - ([Time].PrevMember, Sales)
```

> *"*

2 Comparing values between years

So far, so good. Our expression:

```
(Time.CurrentMember, Measures.Sales) -
(Time.CurrentMember.PrevMember, Measures.Sales)
```

is working fine except that it is producing several negative numbers. If this was a real company we would be concerned with finding out whether there was an explanation for these other than the obvious one that sales are bad.

> *However, we would like to make it clear that we would never use the power of calculated members to, for example, massage the sales figures just to save our jobs; nor would we condone this action in others. Obviously.*

One explanation for the variable figures may be that our sales are seasonal, so in July we see that we sold fewer items than in June, but perhaps that's an effect of the summer silly season. Perhaps we always sell fewer items in

July. Is there a way to compare a member not to the previous member, but to the parallel period? That is to say, can we compare the sales in January with the January sales from the previous year? Can we compare the Quarter 1 sales with the previous year's Quarter 1 sales and so on?

Answer: of course there is (otherwise we would never have brought up the problem in the first place). In this case we want to start once more with:

```
Time.CurrentMember, Measures.Sales
```

and to think first about members at the Month level. We know about the Lag function, so we could try:

```
Time.CurrentMember.Lag(12), Measures.Sales
```

Wherever we are in the month dimension, we're going to get the month from the previous year. Does this work?

```
(Time.CurrentMember, Measures.Sales) -
(Time.CurrentMember.Lag(12), Measures.Sales)
```

Create it as a calculated measure and see. The answer is "Yes! It works! Well... up to a point."

- Quarter	Month	MeasuresLevel Sales	Lag Growth
1997 Total		$565,238.13	$565,238.13
	Q1 Total	$139,628.35	$139,628.35
- Q1	1	$45,539.69	$45,539.69
	2	$44,058.79	$44,058.79
	3	$50,029.87	$50,029.87
+ Q2	Q2 Total	$132,666.27	$132,666.27
+ Q3	Q3 Total	$140,271.89	$140,271.89
+ Q4	Q4 Total	$152,671.62	$152,671.62
1998 Total		$1,079,147.47	$1,079,147.47
	Q1 Total	$290,873.18	$290,873.18
- Q1	1	$98,155.28	$52,615.59
	2	$94,498.00	$50,439.21
	3	$98,219.90	$48,190.03
	Q2 Total	$287,009.99	$287,009.99
- Q2	4	$94,776.14	$51,897.89
	5	$95,183.81	$50,727.52
	6	$97,050.04	$51,718.31
+ Q3	Q3 Total	$295,040.55	$295,040.55
+ Q4	Q4 Total	$206,223.75	$206,223.75

It works at the month level for the year 1998. It doesn't work for months in 1997, but that's because we don't have the necessary comparative data from 1996 so we can't blame the expression for that. However, at the Quarter level, Lag(12) is 12 quarters ago (which is three years back) and at the year level the expression is trying to compare with data from twelve years ago. This expression is a good first attempt, but it doesn't fully answer the question: we want to compare to just one year ago and we want the expression to work at all levels. You will not be surprised at this point to discover that we have a function up our sleeve(s) called `ParallelPeriod` in MDX.

`ParallelPeriod` takes three parameters. The first tells it the time span you want to go back for comparison; in other words, what you mean by period. We have `Year`, `Quarter` and `Month` as our periods, each equating to a level in the hierarchy and in this case we're talking about performing comparisons with data that comes from the previous year, so we put `Year` as the first parameter.

The second parameter is simply a numeric expression; the function is saying "tell me how many of these time units you want to go back". In our case, the value we need is '1' because we want to compare with data from one year back.

The last parameter tells the function which member to work upon and so we use `CurrentMember` again because we want it to work not just at the month level but at the quarter and year levels as well.

The first part of our expression is fine so we write:

```
(Time.CurrentMember, Measures.Sales) -
(ParallelPeriod(Year,1,Time.CurrentMember)
```

and we're looking for the `Sales` measure, so the complete expression reads:

```
(Time.CurrentMember, Measures.Sales) -
(ParallelPeriod(Year,1,Time.CurrentMember), Measures.Sales)
```

and that's our answer. Try it for yourself as a calculated measure called PP Growth.

- Quarter	Month	MeasuresLevel	
		Sales	PP Growth
1997 Total		$565,238.13	$565,238.13
	Q1 Total	$139,628.35	$139,628.35
- Q1	1	$45,539.69	$45,539.69
	2	$44,058.79	$44,058.79
	3	$50,029.87	$50,029.87
+ Q2	Q2 Total	$132,666.27	$132,666.27
+ Q3	Q3 Total	$140,271.89	$140,271.89
+ Q4	Q4 Total	$152,671.62	$152,671.62
1998 Total		$1,079,147.47	$513,909.34
	Q1 Total	$290,873.18	$151,244.83
- Q1	1	$98,155.28	$52,615.59
	2	$94,498.00	$50,439.21
	3	$98,219.90	$48,190.03
	Q2 Total	$287,009.99	$154,343.72
- Q2	4	$94,776.14	$51,897.89
	5	$95,183.81	$50,727.52
	6	$97,050.04	$51,718.31
+ Q3	Q3 Total	$295,040.55	$154,768.66
+ Q4	Q4 Total	$206,223.75	$53,552.13

Excellent.

3 Calculating values to date

Let's look at another problem. Lots of people ask "What are my sales from the beginning of the year till now?" We'll solve this in two stages. The first is to find all of the appropriate values and the second is to aggregate those values to provide the total to date.

For the first stage we need a function called YTD (which stands for YearToDate). YTD is actually the equivalent of another function called PeriodsToDate, and PeriodsToDate is similar to ParallelPeriod in that you specify the unit of time you're looking at; in other words, which level defines the period in your expression. YTD is more specific in that it's always going to look at the current year and say "Give me a member and I'll return to you a set that includes that member plus all the previous members at that level which are still within that year."

The member that interests us is Time.CurrentMember. Wherever we are, we want to get back a set of members (months or quarters) that came before the current member in the current year, and the set should include the current member. So, if we were looking at March 2000, the YTD function would return January 2000, February 2000 and March 2000. We start writing the expression for a calculated member called YTD like this:

```
(YTD(Time.CurrentMember),
```

❝ *Note that this YTD function, unlike the previous ones we have looked at, isn't simply returning numerical data. Instead it is returning a set that consists of members from the same dimension.* ❞

Once we have the set returned by YTD we can perform whatever operations we like upon it. In this case we want to aggregate the data so we use the Sum function.

Sum takes two parameters, the first of which, conveniently enough, is a set. We have our set as provided by the YTD function so we put that in:

```
Sum(YTD(Time.CurrentMember),
```

The second parameter required by Sum is a numeric expression: that's the measure that we're interested in, Sales. So we say "Give me the sum of the set of YTD members for Sales". This is the complete expression:

```
Sum(YTD(Time.CurrentMember), Measures.Sales)
```

The result looks like this:

- Quarter	Month	MeasuresLevel	
		Sales	YTD
1997 Total		$565,238.13	$565,238.13
	Q1 Total	$139,628.35	$139,628.35
- Q1	1	$45,539.69	$45,539.69
	2	$44,058.79	$89,598.48
	3	$50,029.87	$139,628.35
+ Q2	Q2 Total	$132,666.27	$272,294.62
+ Q3	Q3 Total	$140,271.89	$412,566.51
+ Q4	Q4 Total	$152,671.62	$565,238.13
1998 Total		$1,079,147.47	$1,079,147.47
	Q1 Total	$290,873.18	$290,873.18
- Q1	1	$98,155.28	$98,155.28
	2	$94,498.00	$192,653.28
	3	$98,219.90	$290,873.18
	Q2 Total	$287,009.99	$577,883.17
- Q2	4	$94,776.14	$385,649.32
	5	$95,183.81	$480,833.13
	6	$97,050.04	$577,883.17
+ Q3	Q3 Total	$295,040.55	$872,923.72
+ Q4	Q4 Total	$206,223.75	$1,079,147.47

Summary

You have now written your first MDX expressions and met a few very useful functions, such as the perennially useful CurrentMember. This function, together with PrevMember and NextMember, are invaluable for identifying where you want to be within a cube.

You've also written MDX code incorporating these and other functions to create calculated members, or calculated measures to be even more precise. Clearly you have to balance the pros and cons before deciding to use a calculated measure in your particular cube, but you'll have guessed by now that we are encouraging you to use them in many cases. They are often an excellent solution when the value for the new measure is derivable from the existing measures.

We've had to cover a lot of groundwork and theory to reach this point but if you're still with us, you've made a good start towards mastery of basic MDX. There's a lot to grasp, especially from a standing start, so several passes may help you tighten your grip. We'd recommend reviewing the previous few chapters if the groundwork ever begins to feel a little shaky or if you need to refresh your understanding.

The table below lists the functions we've covered in this chapter, showing what they require and what they return.

Function	Requires	Returns
CurrentMember	Dimension	Member
PrevMember	Member	Member
NextMember	Member	Member
Lag	Numeric expression	Member
Lead	Numeric expression	Member
ParallelPeriod	Level, numeric expression, member	Set
YTD	Member	Set
Sum	Set, numeric expression	Number

Chapter 6

Navigating the hierarchy

Resources:

Starting database – FoodMart2000_MDX1
Cube – Sales_MDX1
Completed sample database – FoodMart2000_EndChap7
MDX samples – CHAP6.TXT

We talked in the last chapter about relative referencing of cells in a cube. CurrentMember is very useful as a dynamic "you are here" identifier for a particular cell, both when used on its own and in conjunction with other functions such as PrevMember, Lag and Lead.

However, there are also times when it is useful to be able to refer to members by means of their position within the hierarchy of a particular dimension, and in this chapter we'll explore relative referencing of members.

A hierarchy can also be called a family tree. This is an apposite term, matching the way that MDX references members within a hierarchy: familiar words like parents, children, descendants and ancestors are used which will need little explanation.

The illustrations below shows the hierarchy of the Time and Product dimensions in SALES_MDX1. You've already met these in passing, and here we are going to use them to illustrate some of the tools available to you for navigating a hierarchy.

Here are the levels in both dimensions:

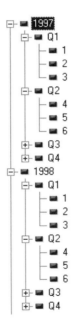

Here are some sample members in the Time dimension:

and these are some sample members in the Product dimension:

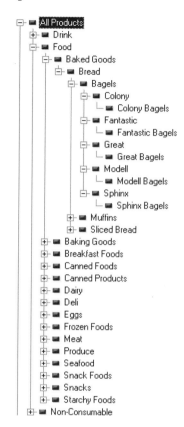

Children

We'll start by looking at parent–child relationships. At the top of the Product tree shown above is the All Products member, which is the only member of the (All) level. Below it are Drink, Food and Non-Consumable, the three members of the Product Family level. As you'd guess, All Products is the parent of all three and they are its children.

The Children function, predictably enough, identifies the member or members one level below the starting level. You specify the member for which you wish the children returned and then invoke the Children function.

So:

```
[Product].[All Products].Children
```

returns the set of all three members of the level immediately beneath the (All) level, namely Drink, Food and Non-Consumable.

❝ *Incidentally, if you are really keen you can insert this kind of statement into an MDX query of a generalized type such as:*

```
SELECT
{[Product].[All Products].Children} ON COLUMNS
FROM [Sales_MDX1]
```

to see that it does work and to check what it will return. For this reason, all of these statements are in the Chap6.txt file; just in case you want to try them out. ❞

Similarly, the expression:

```
[Time].[1997].Children
```

returns all four members at the level immediately beneath the 1997 member, namely Q1, Q2, Q3 and Q4.

There are two variations on the theme of children: FirstChild and LastChild. As you might expect from the family tree analogy,

```
[Time].[1997].FirstChild
```

will return Q1 and

```
[Time].[1997].LastChild
```

will return Q4.

Parent

To no-one's great surprise, the Parent function works the other way around. So given the expression:

```
[Product].[All Products].[Drink].Parent
```

the Parent function would return the All Products member.

If we use a different child of All Products:

```
[Product].[All Products].[Food].Parent
```

the Parent function still returns the All Products member in exactly the same way.

And, just like the `Child` function, we can use `Parent` at any level of the hierarchy, so:

    [Time].[1997].[Q1].[1].Parent

will return `[Time].[1997].[Q1]` as the parent member.

❛ *Note that there is an important difference between `Children` and `Parent`. `Children` returns a set while `Parent` returns a single member. However, as long as you wrap these up in curly brackets they will still work in an MDX query, for example:*

```
SELECT
{[Time].[1997].[Q1].[1].Parent} ON COLUMNS
FROM [Sales_MDX1]
```

Incidentally, during proof-reading Mosha added the following. "It is also important to avoid confusion between tuples and members in this chapter. A member is always also a tuple, but a tuple is not always a member. Therefore, a member can be used anywhere where tuples can be used, but not vice versa. For example, functions like `Parent` will work on a member, i.e. `USA.Parent`, but won't work on a tuple, i.e. `(USA, Drink).Parent` will return an error." This is an excellent point and worth bearing in mind when you first play with functions because it is easy to get confused between the two. Of course, after a while it will become second nature. ❜

Nesting functions

As you might imagine, you can nest the functions so you can ask for:

    [Product].[All Products].LastChild.Children

which returns `Carousel, Checkout, Health and Hygiene, Household` and `Periodicals`.

or:

    [Product].[All Products].LastChild.Parent

which returns `All Products`.

However, you can't use something like:

    [Product].[All Products].Children.Parent

which is logical enough because `[Product].[All Products].Children` returns a set but `Parent` is expecting a member.

Outside the limits

If you ask for the Parent of a top level member, or the Child of a bottom level one, then the functions return NULL members (rather than a zero).

❻ *Incidentally, the concept of NULL members is very important and very different from zero. Zero is a number, but the Parent function always returns a member. So MDX has a concept of a special NULL member which is always returned when functions go out of bounds. For example:*

```
[Products].[All Products].FirstChild.Parent
```

returns [Products].[All Products]

But

```
[Products].[All Products].Parent.FirstChild
```

returns NULL, because Parent took us outside the limits. ❾

Reality check

At this point you may be thinking "Well, this is all interesting enough but to write the MDX expression to return the parent of Drink, we had to drill down through the parent itself which means we had to know the parent before we started." True. Good point. But, like all programming languages, synergy always comes into play – the whole is greater than the sum of the parts. For example, try combining the Parent function with CurrentMember to create a calculated measure called, say, Product Percentage:

```
(Product.CurrentMember, Measures.[Unit Sales]) /
(Product.CurrentMember.Parent, Measures.[Unit Sales]) * 100
```

This shows us the unit sales for any given member expressed as a percentage of the unit sales of its parent. This apparently innocent expression turns out to be deceptively powerful.

Take a look at the breakfast foods part of the Product dimension, shown below.

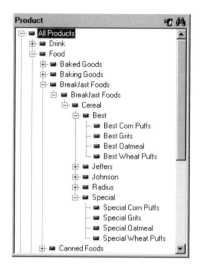

Our new calculated measure lets us drill up and down the product hierarchy and see how each group is doing in comparison to its siblings (children of the same parent).

It can tell us, for instance, what percentage of unit sales were generated by each of the five breakfast cereal manufacturers.

❧ *If you want to see this in ProClarity, fire it up and connect to the cube. Click on the Dimensions button in the toolbar, click on the measures tab that appears and select your new calculated measure. (If you can't see it, check you've saved the new measure in the Cube Editor and try refreshing the view from ProClarity by selecting File, Open Cube.) Then drag and drop dimensions between the Rows, Columns and Background boxes until they are as shown. Select the Product tab, drill down and select the products as shown in the following illustration. Finally, press the Execute button.* ❦

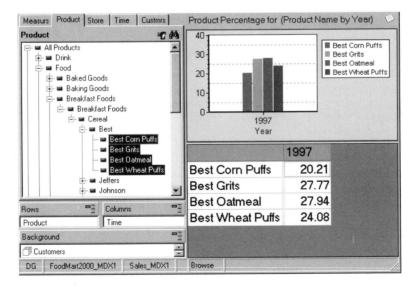

It also shows which of the Best range of products performed as its brand name suggests, and can also compare the sales of Best and Special products.

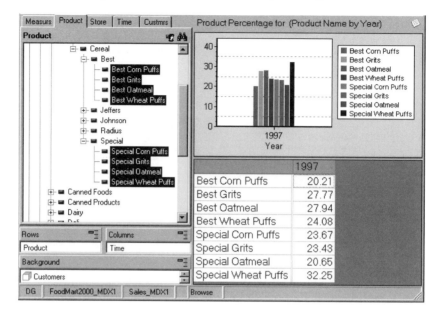

Special Wheat Puffs seem to have an edge...

Furthermore, you can make use of the fact that you know the name of the top member and create a calculated measure called, say, Product Total Percentage:

```
(Product.CurrentMember, Measures.[Unit Sales]) /
(Product.[All Products], Measures.[Unit Sales]) * 100
```

which will give you, at any level, the percentage of total unit sales that are due to a particular member, rather than an absolute unit sales figure.

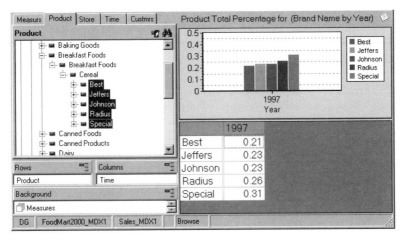

So a query like:

```
SELECT
{ [Time].[1997] } ON COLUMNS ,
{ [Product].[All Products].Children} ON ROWS
FROM [Sales_MDX1]
WHERE ( [Measures].[Product Total Percentage] )
```

is very effective.

However, it rapidly gets very tedious when you want to select a large number of members at the lower levels of the hierarchy. What we need here is a function that will find descendants for us....

Descendants

Regrettably there is no Grandchildren function but we do have at our disposal a very powerful function called Descendants.

The Descendants function normally requires you to supply two arguments – a member and then the level at which you wish to retrieve the set of descendants, for example:

```
Descendants( [Time].[1997],[Quarter])
```

Note the comma that sits between the member and the level, and the braces that wrap around the arguments that the Descendants function requires.

 Arguments are the stuff that some functions need in order to... err... function; they're often wrapped up in some way and MDX uses braces for its wrappings. Some functions take arguments, as does Descendants, and some, like Parent, don't. ❩

In the expression above, we're looking at the Time dimension, the 1997 member and at the Quarter level. This expression would return the set of descendants of 1997 at the Quarter level, namely the four quarters Q1, Q2, Q3 and Q4.

The expression:

```
Descendants( [Time].[1998],[Month])
```

would return all twelve months 1, 2, 3, 4, 5, 6, 7, 8, 9, 10, 11 and 12 (that is, all the descendants of 1998 at the month level) and:

```
Descendants( [Time].[1998].[Q2],[Month])
```

would return all the descendants of Q2 at the month level, namely 4, 5 and 6.

Descendants can also take a different second argument: the first is still the member in which you're interested and this time the second is the number of levels you want to go down in the hierarchy. To get the same result as the previous expression, you'd write:

```
Descendants( [Time].[1998].[Q2],1)
```

And, to get all twelve months we could also use:

```
Descendants( [Time].[1998],2)
```

If we failed to specify the level by leaving the final element out of the expression, like this:

```
Descendants( [Time].[1998].[Q2])
```

it would still work but it would return Q2 itself and also 4, 5 and 6. In other words, without the final part of the argument that specifies the level from which members should be returned, Descendants will return the stated member and all members at any level below it in the hierarchy.

So:

```
Descendants( [Time].[1997])
```

returns 1997, Q1, Q2, Q3, Q4,1, 2, 3, 4, 5, 6, 7, 8, 9, 10, 11 and 12. At first sight this appears relatively unhelpful – rather a mixed bag of members, in fact. But in practice it turns out to be very useful. For example, when combined with the Product Total Percentage calculated measure that you created earlier, you can now write an MDX query like:

```
SELECT
{Descendants( [Time].[1997])} ON COLUMNS ,
{[Product].Children } ON ROWS
FROM [Sales_MDX1]
WHERE ( [Measures].[Product Total Percentage] )
```

which allows you, at a glance, to compare sales of product groups both by quarter and by month.

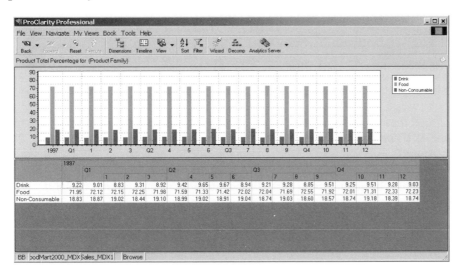

In fact, if you drill a little deeper with:

```
SELECT
{Descendants( [Time].[1997])} ON COLUMNS ,
{[Product].[Product Family].[Food].[Breakfast
Foods].[Breakfast Foods].[Cereal].Children } ON ROWS
FROM [Sales_MDX1]
WHERE ( [Measures].[Product Total Percentage] )
```

You find:

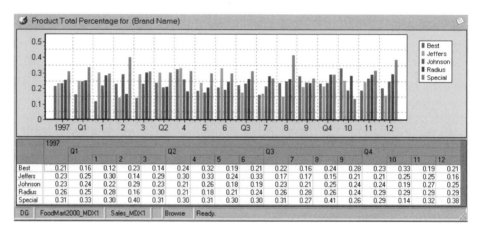

Sadly we can't show this graph in color, when it works much better and shows plainly that Special products sell really well in February, August and December.

What happens if you ask for the descendants of a member that has no descendants? The expression will still work, and it will return just the member you've specified. If you wrote:

```
Descendants([Time].[1997].[Q1].[1])
```

just the [1] member itself (that is, January) would be returned.

❡ *You will find when browsing the help system that many of the functions we introduce have even more flexibility and power than we are describing here. The De-scendants function, for instance, can have any one of seven so called 'desc_flags' set in order to modify its behavior from the plain vanilla default that we describe in this chapter. As we said in the introduction, we don't feel it's always helpful to load you with detail when that extra information is readily available once you've got over the initial learning curve.* ❡

Reality check

To overcome the tedious selection problem discussed above, we can now use a query like:

```
SELECT
{ [Time].[1997] } ON COLUMNS ,
{ Descendants([Product].[All Products],3)} ON ROWS
FROM [Sales_MDX1]
WHERE ( [Measures].[Product Total Percentage] )
```

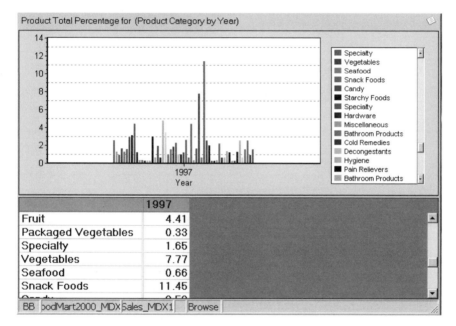

❡ *In case you were wondering, that tall spike is Snack Foods and the next tallest one is Vegetables.* **❡**

and all we have to do is to change the 3 to 4 or 5 to drill further and further down. We can even use a 6 and drill right down to the individual products.

Product Total Percentage for (Product Name by Year)	
	1997
Better Canned Tuna in Oil	0.06
Better Canned Tuna in Water	0.07
Blue Label Canned Tuna in Oil	0.05
Blue Label Canned Tuna in Water	0.07
Bravo Canned Tuna in Oil	0.06
Bravo Canned Tuna in Water	0.06
Just Right Canned Tuna in Oil	0.08
Just Right Canned Tuna in Water	0.08
Pleasant Canned Tuna in Oil	0.05
Pleasant Canned Tuna in Water	0.06
Better Canned Beets	0.05
Better Canned Peas	0.07
Better Canned String Beans	0.06
Better Canned Tomatos	0.06
Better Canned Yams	0.06
Better Creamed Corn	0.07
Blue Label Canned Beets	0.05
Blue Label Canned Peas	0.07
Blue Label Canned String Beans	0.05
Blue Label Canned Tomatos	0.06

❧ *There is so much data in the cube once you're looking four or more levels down that ProClarity can only display the data as a grid. And, be warned, this query may take some time to execute because it drills down so far!* ❧

Ancestor

The Descendants function lets you work downwards within a hierarchy and, as you might expect, there is a similar function to work upwards within a hierarchy – Ancestor. Like Descendants it takes arguments: the first is the member in which you're interested and the second is the level at which you want to find the ancestors of the chosen member. In the Products dimension again, the expression:

```
Ancestor( [Product].[All Products].[Food].[Baked
Goods].[Bread].[Bagels], [Product Department])
```

works back from the Bagels member to find the corresponding ancestral member at the Product Department level. That happens to be the member Baked Goods which is what the function returns.

As with Descendants, Ancestor can also take a numeric second argument that specifies the number of levels you want to go up in the hierarchy. To get the same result as the previous expression, you'd write:

```
Ancestor( [Product].[All Products].[Food].[Baked
Goods].[Bread].[Bagels], 2)
```

and if you wrote:

```
Ancestor( [Product].[All Products].[Food].[Baked
Goods].[Bread].[Bagels], 3)
```

it would take you one step further back, to the Product Family level and the member Food. To reach this level by specifying the level by name rather than by number of steps through the hierarchy, you'd write:

```
Ancestor([Product].[All Products].[Food].[Baked
Goods].[Bread].[Bagels], [Product Family])
```

and the result would still be the member Food.

Siblings

Having scaled the heights and plumbed the depths of a hierarchy with the Ancestor and Descendants functions, we'll finish by introducing a further two close relations: Sibling and Cousin.

In human terms, a sibling is a brother or a sister and within a hierarchy it means the set of members at the same level who share the same parent. You specify the member for which you want to find siblings and follow it by the Sibling function, like this:

```
[Product].[All Products].[Food].[Baked
Goods].[Bread].[Bagels].Siblings
```

returns Bagels, Muffins and Sliced Bread. Note that the specified member (Bagels), being by definition one of the collection of siblings, is part of the set of members returned.

The functions FirstSibling and LastSibling work in the same way as FirstChild and LastChild:

```
[Product].[All Products].[Food].[Baked
Goods].[Bread].[Bagels].FirstSibling
```

returns Bagels – being the first member listed in the level, the Bagels member is its own first sibling.

```
[Product].[All Products].[Food].[Baked
Goods].[Bread].[Bagels].LastSibling
```

returns Sliced Bread, being the last member in the level containing Bagels.

Cousin

Finally, there's the Cousin function. This works best when there is always the same number of siblings within a level. The Time dimension is often like this: years always have four quarters, and quarters always have three months. January in Q1 is the first month in the quarter and is, for the purposes of this function, deemed to be a cousin of the other three months that come first in the other quarters, i.e. January is a cousin of April in Q2, July in Q3 and October in Q4. You use this function by first specifying the member for which you want to locate a cousin and then the parent member for which the cousin is to be found. This sounds complicated, but is easy in practice. For example:

    Cousin([Time].[1998].[Q1].[1], [Q2])

returns [Time].[1998].[Q2].[4] because January's cousin in Q2 is April.

    Cousin([Time].[1998].[Q4], [1997])

returns Q4 in 1997.

Having symmetrical levels in a dimension is vital to the predictable use of the Cousin function as the position of each member determines which other members it can call cousin.

Summary

Sadly there are no Aunt or Uncle functions to play with, so that brings us to the end of the functions that let you use relative referencing to navigate a hierarchy. These functions provide flexible short cuts to moving around a hierarchy and armed with this knowledge, you should now be able to navigate a hierarchy in a relative fashion.

Once again, here is a table listing the functions from this chapter, showing what they require and what they return.

Function	Requires	Returns
Parent	Member	Member
Children	Member	Set
FirstChild	Member	Member
LastChild	Member	Member
Descendants	Member, level or Member, distance	Set
Ancestor	Member, level or Member, distance	Member
Siblings	Member	Set
FirstSibling	Member	Member
LastSibling	Member	Member
Cousin	Member, ancestor member	Member

For your entertainment, below are MDX queries that use some of the expressions we have introduced in this chapter. You can either look at them and try and work out what they will return, or you can cut and paste them from the Chap6.txt file into your front-end tool to see what they do.

```
SELECT
{[Time].[1997] } ON COLUMNS,
Descendants( [Product].[Bread],[Product Subcategory]) ON ROWS
FROM [Sales_MDX1]
WHERE ( [Measures].[Unit Sales] )

SELECT
{[Time].[1997] } ON COLUMNS,
Descendants( [Product].[Bread]) ON ROWS
FROM [Sales_MDX1]
WHERE ( [Measures].[Unit Sales] )

SELECT
{ Cousin([Time].[1],[Q2]) } ON COLUMNS ,
{ [Product].[All Products] } ON ROWS
FROM [Sales_MDX1]

SELECT
{ Descendants([Time].[1998].[Q1].[1],[Month]) } ON COLUMNS ,
{ [Customers].[All Customers] } ON ROWS
FROM [Sales_MDX1]
WHERE ( [Measures].[Unit Sales] )
```

```
SELECT
{ [Product].[All Products] } ON COLUMNS ,
{[Time].[1997].[Q1].Parent } ON ROWS
FROM [Sales_MDX1]

SELECT
{ [Time].[1997] } ON COLUMNS ,
{ Descendants(Product,[Product Category]) } ON ROWS
FROM [Sales_MDX1]
WHERE ( [Measures].[Product Percentage] )

SELECT
{ Descendants([Time].[1997],Month) } ON COLUMNS ,
{ [Customers].[All Customers] } ON ROWS
FROM [Sales_MDX1]
WHERE ( [Measures].[Unit Sales] )

SELECT
{ [Time].[1997] } ON COLUMNS ,
{ Descendants(Product,[Product Category]) } ON ROWS
FROM [Sales_MDX1]
WHERE ( [Measures].[Product Total Percentage] )

SELECT
{ Descendants( [Time])} ON COLUMNS ,
{ DESCENDANTS( [Product].[All Products],
[Product].[Product Department] ) } ON ROWS
FROM [Sales_MDX1]
WHERE ( [Measures].[Product Total Percentage] )
```

Chapter 7

Snapshot data analysis

Resources:

Starting database – `FoodMart2000_MDX1`
Cube – `Sales_MDX1A`
Completed sample database – `FoodMart2000_EndChap7`
MDX samples – `CHAP7.TXT`

The MDX functions covered in the last two chapters are more than enough to get you started on your glittering career solving OLAP cube problems (or meeting OLAP cube challenges, if you prefer). In this chapter we'll look at some business problems that are common to inventory systems and, of course, we'll also cover how to cure them. They happen to be well suited to inventory type problems but, of course, they have many wider applications. *(The sub-text here is "Even if you don't happen to work with inventories, these functions are still worth getting to know!")*

We'll be working with more of MDX's functions so this seems like a good time to talk about what they require in order to work, and what they return. This becomes important when you start writing expressions using multiple functions. Functions like `Descendants` and `Children` return a set and others, like `CurrentMember` or `Parent`, return a member. If you use the `Descendants` function to find the sales figures for all the products of a particular type, for instance, any function you use to further process the resulting set must be able to accept a set as its input. You would, for example, be able to `Sum` the figures or `Count` them (the `Count` function is introduced in this chapter) because both `Sum` and `Count` require a set to work upon.

The take-home message is that you must ensure that each function is given what it wants and as with many things, it becomes easier with practice and as you gain familiarity with the common functions. Nobody is expected to remember the peculiarities of each function – there are well over a hundred of them. That's the task of the MDX Function Reference section in the help system.

The general problem

This time we'll be using the cube called Sales_MDX1A from the FoodMart2000_MDX1 database. This is an inventory cube with three dimensions – Product, Time and Store – and just one measure, Quantity, which is the number of items there are in the warehouse.

By default, an OLAP cube sums values which is very often exactly what you need, but when the values are part of an inventory, this approach doesn't reflect reality at all well, as you can see from the table below.

Year	Quarter	Month	Quantity
2000			790 ✗
	Q1		120 ✗
		January	30
		February	40
		March	50
	Q2		200 ✗
		April	65
		May	45
		June	90
	Q3		185 ✗
		July	55
		August	60
		September	70
	Q4		285 ✗
		October	80
		November	100
		December	105

❝ *The numbers in the table are for illustration; they're not taken from the cube.* ❞

All the totals for quarters and the yearly total are wrong (they're marked with an ✗). You have figures that tell you how many, say, cans of sardines you had in stock at the end of January, February and March but, come the end of the quarter, the sum of those three figures tells you nothing about the state of your stockholding at the end of the first quarter. The value for Q1 should be 50, which is the March total, not 120, which is the sum of the January, February and March totals.

The general solution

Instead of summing everything, we want to see a snapshot of the figures at a particular point in time. We also need to generate some more figures in order for the snapshot to be meaningful.

The specific requirements

So we are going to look at three specific areas:

- Average stockholding – We need to know the average number of items in stock during each time period
- Closing period – We need opening and closing balances for the period
- Max and Min – We want the maximum and minimum stockholding levels.

❢ *For each of the first two we're going to show you two solutions – a 'brute force', inelegant one and an elegant one. Ultimately of course, in a real situation, we'd use the elegant solution. So why are we bothering to show you the inelegant one? Well, it isn't just perversity on our part; we're using these requirements to introduce MDX, so the more solutions we can show you, the more MDX we can teach you. And each of the functions that we introduce in the inelegant solutions is seriously useful in its own right.* ❧

There are MDX functions to deal with all of these requirements (no surprises there) so let's start with generating figures for average stockholdings. We do this by creating new calculated members, just as we did in Chapter 5. The process of creating calculated members is not covered again here but you can always flip back to that chapter if you need a refresher.

The recommended method of building expressions is to break any problem down into small elements, then build each of those pieces in MDX before putting them all together to form the whole expression. Setting out your approach in a concise English sentence or two and/or in pseudo-code before writing any MDX are other useful steps which can help you organize your thoughts.

1 Average stockholding

Our first calculated member will be called Average Stock. To find the average stockholding, we need to take the sum of the quantities for all months in the period and divide it by the number of months in the period. In Chapter 2 we explained that MDX 'knows' about cube structures, and this is a good example of the usefulness of that built-in knowledge. When we say period, MDX knows that we have, for example, a quarter level and therefore a period can be defined or constrained by quarters, and this knowledge is going to come in handy when we start writing expressions, which we'll do now.

We'll start with a plain English description of what we want to do:

We take the quantity for each month in the period, sum them and divide the result by the number of months in the period.

Now we can write a tighter description in pseudo-code, a step that's often helpful for getting your approach lined up:

```
Sum(months in the period, Quantity) /
Count(months in the period)
```

Consider the 'months in the period' element: in this case, the period in question is a quarter and there will always be three months in each quarter. The Descendants function, introduced in the last chapter, looks as if it would fit the bill nicely here. We want the Descendants of Time at the CurrentMember,

```
Descendants(Time.CurrentMember)
```

and the CurrentMember must be at the Month level, so we force it to look at the Month level and this is the first fragment of our expression:

```
Descendants(Time.CurrentMember,[Month])
```

Descendants returns a set containing the three months in the period. So, we now know where to look for the values, and now we need to identify the values themselves as coming from the Quantity measure:

```
Measures.Quantity
```

We want to sum the values we've just identified, so we'll use the Sum function. Generically, the Sum function requires two parameters:

```
Sum(Set, Numeric Expression)
```

which is remarkably handy because Descendants returns a set and Measures.Quantity provides the numerical value:

```
Sum(Descendants(Time.CurrentMember,[Month]),
Measures.Quantity)
```

Sum will return a number which we want to divide by another number, namely the number of months in the quarter. The division process is specified with the usual / operator.

```
Sum(Descendants(Time.CurrentMember,[Month]),
Measures.Quantity) /
```

For the second number, we identify the months with the Descendants function just as we did in the first part of the expression, but this time we want to count up how many months there are, instead of finding the sum of the Quantity for each. This we do with another useful function, Count.

```
Sum(Descendants(Time.CurrentMember,[Month]),
Measures.Quantity) / Count(Descendants(
Time.CurrentMember,[Month]))
```

❦ *In this case, Count will always return three because that's the number of months in a quarter.* ❧

So that's our first expression and we can use it to create a calculated measure called Average Stock or AS1 for short.

		MeasuresLevel	
- Quarter	Month	Quantity	AS1
1997 Total		86837	7236
	Q1 Total	21588	7196
- Q1	1	7034	7034
	2	6844	6844
	3	7710	7710
	Q2 Total	20368	6789
- Q2	4	6590	6590
	5	6866	6866
	6	6912	6912
	Q3 Total	21453	7151
- Q3	7	7752	7752
	8	7038	7038
	9	6663	6663
	Q4 Total	23428	7809
- Q4	10	6479	6479
	11	8232	8232
	12	8717	8717
1998 Total		164558	13713

Good, isn't it? Well, yes, it's OK and it works. However, that "Well" and the "OK" don't sound overly enthusiastic, do they? The problem is that our first attempt lacks elegance. It finds averages by brute mathematics, rather than by making use of the ready-made MDX function called Avg (short for Average). The same expression built using Avg is shorter, neater and easier to understand. With our first attempt, if you hadn't written it yourself (or even if it was your own work but you hadn't seen it for several months) you'd have to identify the various elements and work out how they were being used before understanding the whole expression.

<u>Avg works like Sum: it wants a set and a numeric expression.</u> We generate the set as before with the `Descendants` function and the numeric expression is again provided by the `Quantity` measure.

```
Avg(Descendants(Time.CurrentMember,[Month]),
Measures.Quantity)
```

We could describe this in English as "For whichever current member I'm looking at, go to the `Month` level, take the measure `Quantity` for each month and give me the average of those figures."

This one, AS2, is a shorter and more elegant MDX expression.

- Quarter	Month	MeasuresLevel Quantity	AS1	AS2
1997 Total		86837	7236	7236
	Q1 Total	21588	7196	7196
- Q1	1	7034	7034	7034
	2	6844	6844	6844
	3	7710	7710	7710
	Q2 Total	20368	6789	6789
- Q2	4	6590	6590	6590
	5	6866	6866	6866
	6	6912	6912	6912
	Q3 Total	21453	7151	7151
- Q3	7	7752	7752	7752
	8	7038	7038	7038
	9	6663	6663	6663
	Q4 Total	23428	7809	7809
- Q4	10	6479	6479	6479
	11	8232	8232	8232
	12	8717	8717	8717
1998 Total		164558	13713	14960

However, the eagle-eyed amongst you will have noticed that the Average for 1998 (shown as the last row in this screen shot) differs for the two ways of calculating the average. If we drill into this:

1998 Total		164558	13713	14960
+ Q1	Q1 Total	44252	14751	14751
+ Q2	Q2 Total	43849	14616	14616
+ Q3	Q3 Total	44993	14998	14998
	Q4 Total	31464	10488	15732
- Q4	10	14125	14125	14125
	11	17339	17339	17339
	12			

we find that this is because there is no value for December 1998. AS2 is calculating the average based on two months, Average Stock (AS1) is calculating it based on three months because there are three descendants (even if there are not three values associated with them). Exactly how your application should handle this is, of course, up to you and your users, but it is comforting to know that MDX is adaptable enough to give you whichever answer you need.

2 Closing period

OK, that's dealt with average stock, now we'll work on the closing period figure. We want the Quarter 1 total to be the same as the total for March, for Quarter 2 to be the same as June and so on. In fact, we simply want to find the quantity for the last month in the period. We'll call this calculated member Closing Period – CP1.

When writing our first expression we found a good way of identifying all the months and their values:

```
(Descendants(Time.CurrentMember,[Month]), Measures.Quantity)
```

so let's use this again. The only problem is that it returns three numbers, one for each month in the period and we want the last one. Does MDX have anything up its sleeve to help? Yes, and it's a function called Tail.

The Tail function returns one or more items from the end of a set and it always returns its answer in the form of a set. It requires a set to work upon – we can provide that with the code above – and also the number of values you wish it to return.

```
(Tail( Descendants( Time.CurrentMember, [Month]), 1),
Measures.Quantity)
```

Here we've told Tail we want the last member from the set returned by the Descendants function.

Great, it looks as if we are almost there. But first, a couple of questions.

Q. Why are we creating this expression?
A. In order to find a closing period member.
Q. What does the Tail function return?
A. A set. Aah...

Yup, a fatal mismatch error is about to occur. This is an excellent example of why you need to be constantly aware of whether you're dealing with sets or members (or numbers or strings). We need a new function to resolve the potential mismatch by extracting the member from the set, and it's the Item function.

The Item function locates a specific member within a set. Item inspects the members and, in effect, indexes them all. It calls the first item in a set 0, the second 1 and so on. We know the set returned by Tail has but one member, so we want Index to pick up the first and indeed only member. We can see this best if we focus in initially on just the part of the complete expression that uses Tail:

```
Tail( Descendants( Time.CurrentMember, [Month]), 1).Item(0)
```

(Note that the set to be used by the Item function is placed in front of the function name and that there is a dot between the set and the function.)

The complete expression is:

```
(Tail( Descendants( Time.CurrentMember, [Month]), 1).Item(0),
Measures.Quantity)
```

and it works fine.

- Quarter	Month	MeasuresLevel	
		Quantity	CP1
1997 Total		86837	8717
	Q1 Total	21588	7710
- Q1	1	7034	7034
	2	6844	6844
	3	7710	7710
	Q2 Total	20368	6912
- Q2	4	6590	6590
	5	6866	6866
	6	6912	6912
	Q3 Total	21453	6663
- Q3	7	7752	7752
	8	7038	7038
	9	6663	6663
	Q4 Total	23428	8717
- Q4	10	6479	6479
	11	8232	8232
	12	8717	8717
1998 Total		164558	

❡ *There is, as discussed, no closing balance for 1998 as yet; it will appear when data for December 1998 is entered.* ❡

So, it works, but a short cut is open to us: we can use another of MDX's ready-made functions, ClosingPeriod. The ClosingPeriod function needs to know the level and the member in which you're interested – in this case, Month and Time.CurrentMember respectively. Given that information, ClosingPeriod will return the last member found at the specified level. The expression would look like this:

```
(ClosingPeriod([Month], Time.CurrentMember),
Measures.Quantity)
```

The result is exactly the same but the expression itself is more readable and more elegant.

The OpeningBalance function works in the same way except it returns the first member found at the specified level.

3 Maximum value

The third problem is how to get the maximum value for a period; this will be a calculated member called Max For Period, or MaxFP for short. We'll use our tried and tested method of identifying all the months and their values:

    (Descendants(Time.CurrentMember,[Month]), Measures.Quantity)

and combine it with a function called Max (Maximum), which, when given a set and a numeric expression, will return the largest value from that set. The Descendants function provides the set, Measures.Quantity provides the numeric expression and so this code:

    Max(Descendants(Time.CurrentMember, Month), Measures.Quantity)

will do what we want.

Below we can see that the maximum stockholding for the second quarter is the June total and for the third quarter, it's the July figure:

❛ *The* Min *(Minimum) function works in the same way except it returns the smallest value from the set.*

    Min(Descendants(Time.CurrentMember, Month), Measures.Quantity)

❜

Month	MeasuresLevel Quantity	MaxFP	MinFP
	86837	8717	6479
Q1 Total	21588	7710	6844
1	7034	7034	7034
2	6844	6844	6844
3	7710	7710	7710
Q2 Total	20368	6912	6590
4	6590	6590	6590
5	6866	6866	6866
6	6912	6912	6912
Q3 Total	21453	7752	6663
7	7752	7752	7752
8	7038	7038	7038
9	6663	6663	6663
Q4 Total	23428	8717	6479
10	6479	6479	6479
11	8232	8232	8232
12	8717	8717	8717
	164558	17339	14125

Why use Descendants?

Right at the beginning of this chapter we made the decision to use the Descendants function in the new calculated members. You might wonder whether we could, or why we didn't, use the Children function instead. The answer is that we could, but if we did it would be answering a different question because of the different way in which the functions work.

Descendants has the flexibility to return information about, say, the Max value for a **month**, no matter where we are in the cube.

Children will always be relative to a member so for Children to work, we would have to say "give me the Children at the Quarter level", which would return the months, but the expression wouldn't work if we were at the Year level instead of the Quarter level. The expression would have been hard-coded to work with Quarters only.

By using Descendants in combination with the CurrentMember function, we are able to write the expression so that it will behave dynamically. Wherever attention is focused, the function is directed to the Month level and hence to the members of the Month level. So even if we are at the year level, we can see the maximum monthly value for that year.

However, depending upon the question you want to ask, there is no reason at all why you can't use the Children function. For example, if you create a calculated member called, say, Max Child, that reads:

```
Max((Time.CurrentMember.Children), Measures.Quantity)
```

it will return the maximum value for the level underneath the current one. At the year level it shows us the maximum quarterly value for that year.

Month	MeasuresLevel	
	Quantity	Max Child
	86837	23428
Q1 Total	21588	7710
1	7034	
2	6844	
3	7710	
Q2 Total	20368	6912
4	6590	
5	6866	
6	6912	
Q3 Total	21453	7752
7	7752	
8	7038	
9	6663	
Q4 Total	23428	8717
10	6479	
11	8232	
12	8717	
	164558	44993

Summary

We've introduced the following new functions in this chapter, including the nifty Item function which is incredibly useful if you have a set and need a member.

Function	Requires	Returns
Sum	Set, numeric expression	Number
Count	Set	Integer
Avg	Set, numeric expression	Number
Tail	Set, count	Set
Item	Set, index number	Member
OpeningBalance	Level, member	Member
ClosingBalance	Level, member	Member
Max	Set, numeric expression	Number
Min	Set, numeric expression	Number

Chapter 8

Moving averages

Resources:

Starting database – FoodMart2000_MDX2
Cube – Sales_MDX2
Completed sample database – FoodMart2000_EndChap11
MDX samples – CHAP8.TXT

Over the last few chapters you've taken several steps along (and up) the MDX learning curve and we've started to open the door to a great deal of functionality. In this chapter we'll continue the progress by looking at moving averages. These are useful analytical tools which can be used to solve very common business problems.

Moving averages are particularly well suited to tracking the behavior of financial indicators such as Nasdaq in the US or the FTSE 100 in the UK, of specific share prices or indeed of any data collected over time. The graph below represents the behavior of the Nasdaq combined composite index over the period of a year.

The line marked A shows the daily figure. (A color rendition of this graph would be really helpful here, but regrettably we're limited to mono-chrome.) There are three additional lines on the graph which represent the moving average of the index over various periods of time. The line labeled B is a ten-day moving average, line C is a fifty-day moving average and line D is a 200-day moving average.

One reason for using moving averages with stock market data is that the market is very volatile and the index changes very rapidly. If we want to improve the chances of catching a trend, we want to smooth out this rapidity of change over a period of time so we can see more general ups and downs rather than short-term blips. Choosing the period over which smoothing is performed is very important, as you can see from the graph above. Looking at line D, the 200-day moving average with its gently curving path, we can see that its peaks and troughs are very shallow: the longer the period over which we take an average, the smoother the line produced. The trade-off here is if you take an average over too long a period, the line will just look flat and it won't help you to see any trends. Looking at line B, the ten-day moving average, it's again hard to spot trends because of the large number of peaks and troughs in an average taken over a shorter period. Experience, experimentation and knowledge of your data will guide you towards determining moving averages that let you see the level of detail you need. I don't know if anybody looking at this graph could predict what will happen next, but that's the idea that drives the use of moving averages with market data.

A simple moving average

Working with the Sales_MDX2 cube from the FoodMart2000_MDX2 database (which we'll be using for this and the next three chapters), we are going to create a very simple moving average. We'll average our sales, using the data in the Unit Sales measure, over a three month period. This means that whichever month we're in currently, we'll want to take the average of that month, the month immediately before it and the month before that. In pseudo-MDX the expression looks like this:

```
Avg({this month, last month, the month before that},
[Measures].[Unit Sales])
```

The data for each month in the set is taken from the unit sales measure.

Let's talk about our game plan and how we are going to approach writing this expression in proper MDX. We know about the Avg function (from the previous chapter) so calculating the average is no problem. We want the current month and the prior two months – and there's a problem brewing with our pseudo-code approach because we are specifying each month individually. There are three months to list in the expression, which is boring enough to write, but if we wanted an average over ten months or 60 days or whatever, writing the expression would be totally tedious. Can we persuade the Lag function (from Chapter 5) to help here?

Lag will take us to a cell that's a specified number of cells back from our current location so on its own it's not quite going to do the trick because we're looking for a series of cells. Happily Lag has some further versatility that we can use here: it can be teamed with a range operator.

A range operator is a colon – : – and works just as it does in an Excel formula like:

```
=SUM(B3:B16)
```

which adds up the values in cells B3 through B16.

So we can say:

```
Time.CurrentMember.Lag(2): Time.CurrentMember
```

which means take the set of cells made up of the cells named and all of the cells in between them. This is extremely useful because the range operator is a shorthand way of identifying large numbers of cells very quickly.

We can create a new calculated member called MA (Moving Average) and the complete expression it uses would look like this:

```
Avg(Time.CurrentMember.Lag(2): Time.CurrentMember,
Measures.[Unit Sales])
```

It starts with the Avg function, identifies a set for it to work upon, and tells it which values to use. If we plot the data with a front-end tool, it looks reasonable:

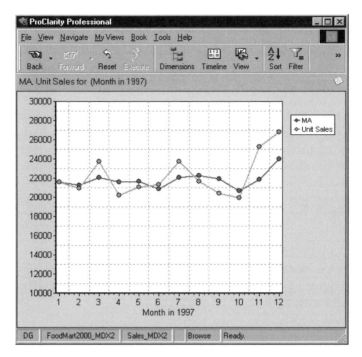

but are we sure that Moving Average is producing the right answers? These are the numbers it produces.

Month 1997	Unit Sales	MA
1	21,628.00	21,628.00
2	20,957.00	21,292.50
3	23,706.00	22,097.00
4	20,179.00	21,614.00
5	21,081.00	21,655.33
6	21,350.00	20,870.00
7	23,763.00	22,064.67
8	21,697.00	**22,270.00**
9	20,388.00	21,949.33
10	19,958.00	20,681.00
11	25,270.00	21,872.00
12	26,796.00	24,008.00

Whip out with your chosen arithmetical assistant (calculator, Pocket PC, abacus, whatever) and check. Sure enough, the Moving Average figure calculated for months 3 to 12 is correct. For example, the figure for month 8 should be:

(21,350.00 + 23,763.00 + 21,697.00)/3 = 66,810/3 = 22,270.

But what about months 1 & 2? Our expression assumes that we are lagging two periods behind. Our data starts with the first month of Q1 of 1997; so what does MDX do when asked to calculate the moving average for January 1997 which has no cells to 'lag' to, and for February 1997 which has only one? Happily, MDX takes the approach that when there are no values, it just does what it can. It doesn't break or sulk, it just uses what's available. Thus, as we can see in the table above, the moving average for January is the same as the unit sales figure because that unit sales figure is all MDX has available. For February, the moving average is calculated by adding the two unit sales figures that are available (those for January and February) and dividing by two. For the March moving average, MDX finally has unit sales figures from three periods to work with and the moving average is calculated exactly as the expression specifies.

The same is true for the quarterly moving averages: the first one calculated from three figures is that for Q3 because this is the first quarter with unit sales figures for two preceding quarters.

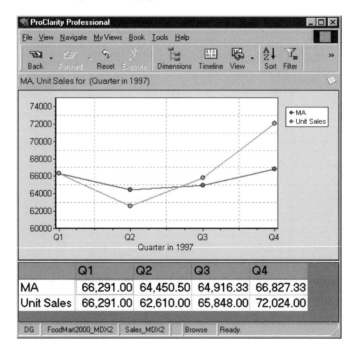

And we only have enough data for the yearly moving average ever to be calculated from two figures, the unit sales totals for 1997 and 1998.

Our expression certainly works, but looked at from a business perspective there is some room for improvement.

A more complex moving average

At present, regardless of where we are in the Time dimension we are lagging two periods and that doesn't always reflect a typical business scenario. While a three-month moving average is sensible enough, a three-day moving average is less likely to be of use. One over thirty days is a more common requirement. Also, a two-quarter moving average might be more appropriate than one generated over three quarters. And finally, in this instance, as we only have values for 1997 and 1998, we actually just want to look at the current year without calculating any moving average over the years.

Let's take a slightly more complex approach to finding a moving average and create a calculated member called CMA (Complex Moving Average). We'll use the formula that we've just defined (shown below) and look again at the way we've used the Lag function.

```
Avg(Time.CurrentMember.Lag(2): Time.CurrentMember,
Measures.[Unit Sales])
```

Ideally we want Lag to act intelligently and to change its behavior depending on where we are in the hierarchy. If we're at the month level, we're happy for it to Lag(2) as it is already doing, but if we're at the quarter level, we want it to Lag(1) to give us a two-quarter moving average and at the year level, we don't want it to lag or calculate anything.

```
If month: Lag(2) : Current
If quarter: Lag(1) : Current
If year: Lag(0) : Current
```

Adding intelligence to the Lag function is going to revolve around a couple of new functions; the first is the Level function. This is a means of finding out where we are in the hierarchy. Level returns the level object for a particular member and its syntax is straightforward. Given our data, the following code:

```
Time.CurrentMember.Level
```

will return either Year, Quarter or Month (being the three levels in the Time dimension), depending on where we are.

The second function we are going to use is the Immediate If function, Iif. This function is by no means unique to MDX, it is found in many computer languages. It's an extremely useful function that we are going to use throughout this chapter. Immediate If takes three parameters, the first of which is a condition to be evaluated. The second parameter tells the function what to do if the condition is met (that is, if it's found to be true) and the third parameter tells the function what to do if the condition is not met (if it's found to be false).

Iif is able to return either a number or a string: here we want it to return a number which will be the number of periods to lag for the current level.

Our Iif function needs to evaluate three possible conditions – whether the level is Month, Quarter or Year. If you haven't used Iif before, you may think that we would need three Iifs to accomplish this, but in fact we can do it with two – one nested inside the other.

The first Iif determines whether we are at the Month level. If this turns out to be true, we want the Lag function to be passed a 2. If it turns out to be false, then logically we must be at either the Quarter or the Year level. So we need another Iif to distinguish between those possibilities and pass the Lag function the appropriate value. This other Iif function is wrapped up (or nested) inside the first, and it asks whether we're at the Quarter level. If the answer to this is "true", Lag is passed a 1, but if the answer is "false" then we must be at the Year level, so we want a zero passed to Lag.

The nested Iif functions look like this:

```
(Iif(Time.CurrentMember.Level is Time.Month, 2,
Iif(Time.CurrentMember.Level is Time.Quarter,1, 0)) )
```

The first one says if the level is month, return the number 2 and the second one says if the level is quarter, return 1 and if the level is neither month nor quarter, return a zero. The number returned by the Iif functions is then fed to the Lag function to tell it how many periods it is to use to calculate the moving average. This is the complete expression:

```
Avg(Time.CurrentMember.Lag
( Iif(Time.CurrentMember.Level is Time.Month,2,
Iif(Time.CurrentMember.Level is Time.Quarter,1, 0)) )
: Time.CurrentMember, Measures.[Unit Sales])
```

❝ *We've split this expression over several lines in the hopes of making it more readable.* ❞

Looking back at our first expression (shown again below for easy comparison) you can see that the (2) that drives the behavior of the Lag function has been replaced by the two nested Iif functions.

```
Avg(Time.CurrentMember.Lag
(2)
: Time.CurrentMember, Measures.[Unit Sales])
```

To the right of those Iif functions in our new expression you'll see the range operator is still present and, just as before, it points to the current member for the Unit Sales measure.

Save the cube and the figures should be as you expect.

Month	MeasuresLevel	
	Unit Sales	CMA
	266,773.00	266,773.00
Q1 Total	66,291.00	66,291.00
1	21,628.00	21,628.00
2	20,957.00	21,292.50
3	23,706.00	22,097.00
Q2 Total	62,610.00	64,450.50
4	20,179.00	21,614.00
5	21,081.00	21,655.33
6	21,350.00	20,870.00
Q3 Total	65,848.00	64,229.00
7	23,763.00	22,064.67
8	21,697.00	22,270.00
9	20,388.00	21,949.33
Q4 Total	72,024.00	68,936.00
10	19,958.00	20,681.00
11	25,270.00	21,872.00
12	26,796.00	24,008.00
	509,987.00	509,987.00

❢ *(This screen shot has been pruned to remove the figures for Sales so that it fits the page better. Your mileage may vary, but no data was harmed in the production of this screen shot.)* ❢

A few moments with your arithmetical assistant should convince you that the expression is doing just what we want and follows the same pattern as before, using as many values as are available in order to fulfill its task.

One last thing – we introduced the Level function so it seems only fair to also mention the Members function, which is very similar. It will work with a dimension or a level and returns a set of member objects.

```
Time.Members
```

returns every member at all levels in the Time dimension.

```
Quarter.Members
```

returns all the members at the Quarter level (Q1 through Q4 twice, once for 1997 and once for 1998).

Summary

Hopefully you're convinced that it's easy to create moving averages in MDX. (If you've ever tried this in SQL you'll know it's a very difficult thing to do.) In order to create moving averages we introduced three new functions: the Level function which returns the location within a hierarchy, the Members function that returns the members from a specified level and the Immediate If or Iif function that's used to define your expression so that it behaves differently depending upon how a condition is evaluated.

Function	Requires	Returns
Level	Member	Level
Members	Level or Dimension	Set
Iif	Condition, what to do if true, what to do if false	Number or string

Chapter 9

Filters

Resources:

Starting database – FoodMart2000_MDX2
Cube – Sales_MDX2
Completed sample database – FoodMart2000_EndChap11
MDX samples – CHAP9.TXT

It is a common requirement to want to extract a subset of the data in a cube depending on whether it meets certain criteria. For instance, you may want to identify any periods in which the sales of many products fell, compared with the sales for the previous period. What we want here is a ratio: we want to take a count of products whose sales fell (when compared to the last period) and divide that by the count of all products. The count of all products with falling sales is a subset of the count of all products and in order to resolve this, MDX has a Filter function which is used to identify subsets of data.

Our approach will be firstly to find out **which** products suffered a drop in sales and then **count** how many such products there are. Next we'll find out how **many** products we have in total and then we'll define a calculated measure to **divide** the product total by the number that fell to produce the ratio, or proportion, of products with sales that fell.

The first part of the description above, where we say we're looking for products that had a drop in sales, should tell you that we're looking for a set.

❥ *As we've said before, it's good to always have a clear idea of what you're dealing with at any point – a set or a member, a number or a string – so that you can ensure you deliver what's expected to the MDX function you're using.* ❥

It should also be clear that the set will be composed of products and that no matter where we are in the product hierarchy, we are looking at products.

That statement should hint to you that we are going to be looking for the CurrentMember at a certain level.

We're working with the Sales_MDX2 cube from the FoodMart2000_MDX2 database. As we can see below, there are seven levels in the Product dimension (if we include the All level) and as we're dealing with individual products here, the one we're interested in is the last one, called Product Name.

In Chapter 6 on navigating the hierarchy we introduced the Descendants function and here we'll use it in earnest to return a set of products. We want it to return the descendants of the current member in the Product dimension at the Product Name level. This is the first step towards our expression:

```
Descendants([Product].CurrentMember, [Product Name])
```

which finds all the products that are below the current member in the hierarchy at the Product Name level.

We are going to build our final expression in stages. In order to reduce the visual complexity of the intermediate steps, we're going to temporarily substitute the text 'SetOfProducts' for the above expression. This is a useful trick when you are building expressions for yourself.

Now we have this set, we want to know how many of them had a drop in sales, so we're now looking for a set within the set we've just identified. This is where the Filter function comes in. It requires a set and a condition to evaluate; once it has evaluated the condition, it will return a subset. In this case, Filter will look at the set of all products and generate a subset. It will inspect the unit sales value of the current member of the Time dimension and, if this value is smaller than the unit sales value of the previous member in the Time dimension, then sales have fallen and it will be included in the subset.

Here's the second step in our expression:

```
Filter(SetOfProducts, ([Time].CurrentMember, [Unit Sales]) <
( [Time].PrevMember, [Unit Sales] ))
```

As we said, 'SetOfProducts' is simply a marker to show where our first expression will go in the finished code. Also, remember that Time.PrevMember is a shortened form of Time.CurrentMember.PrevMember.

Now we have the subset of products which had a drop in sales and need to know how many products the subset contains. For this we can use the Count function, placing it in front of the Filter function:

```
Count(Filter(SetOfProducts, ([Time].CurrentMember,
[Unit Sales]) < ([Time].PrevMember, [Unit Sales])))
```

in order to get a count of the members in the subset.

To finish off the expression we need to count how many products we have in total. That information was contained in the unfiltered set we generated with the Descendants function, so we can use that part of the expression again, preceding it with Count, like this:

```
Count(SetOfProducts)
```

That's the job done, all we have to do is to plug the components together:

```
Count(Filter(SetOfProducts, ([Time].CurrentMember,
[Unit Sales]) < ([Time].PrevMember, [Unit Sales])))
/
Count(SetOfProducts)
```

and finally replace the SetOfProducts marker with the code segment we wrote as the first step.

```
Count(Filter( Descendants([Product].CurrentMember,
[Product Name]),
([Time].CurrentMember, [Unit Sales]) <
([Time].PrevMember, [Unit Sales])))
/
Count(Descendants( [Product].CurrentMember, [Product Name]))
```

The first Count function returns the number of products with sales that fell and the second Count function returns the total number of products, so inserting the divide operator between the Count functions divides the first number by the second.

This will tell us the ratio of products that fell in any period.

❧ *It is worth noting here that if you wanted to support different types of analysis you could define the two* Count *functions as separate calculated measures and then define a third calculated measure that put them together. You'd have three calculated measures: one would give you the count of products with sales that fell, the second would give you the count of all the products in the* Product *dimension and the third one would be the complete expression which generates the ratio of products with a drop in sales.* ❧

Create a new calculated member called Products Down and enter the MDX code, checking to see that it passes the syntax check, and look at the new column of data.

			MeasuresLevel
- Year	- Quarter	Month	Products Down
	1997 Total		0
		Q1 Total	0
	- Q1	1	0
		2	0.503205128205128
		3	0.405128205128205
- 1997		Q2 Total	0.544230769230769
	- Q2	4	0.562179487179487
		5	0.463461538461538
		6	0.469871794871795
	+ Q3	Q3 Total	0.448076923076923
	+ Q4	Q4 Total	0.408974358974359
+ 1998	1998 Total		0

We have every confidence that the expression itself is OK, but the fractions are being expressed to an annoying number of decimal places and we might wonder why some of the data is appearing as zeros – indicating that sales of none of our products fell, which seems unlikely.

The first issue is simply the default display setting. The values we've generated are ratios, and a ratio is another way of describing a percentage. By default the Cube Browser uses the standard number format string for all the numbers it displays. The answer is to change the format string. Highlight the Products Down member in the Tree Pane and then click on the Advanced tab in the Properties display, locate the Format String property:

and, from the pop down the list of formats, select Percent. The Products Down column now looks much more sensible:

- Year	- Quarter	Month	MeasuresLevel Products Down
	1997 Total		0.00%
		Q1 Total	0.00%
	- Q1	1	0.00%
		2	50.32%
		3	40.51%
- 1997		Q2 Total	54.42%
	- Q2	4	56.22%
		5	46.35%
		6	46.99%
	+ Q3	Q3 Total	44.81%
	+ Q4	Q4 Total	40.90%
+ 1998	1998 Total		0.00%

❦ *Bear in mind that we are changing the display format here in Analysis Services, not in your front-end tool. If, for example, you view the new calculated measure from an Excel pivot table, even after you've changed the format string to percent, Excel shows the values as fractions to many decimal places. You have to format the cells in the pivot table itself in order to see the values as percentages. Other front-end tools, like ProClarity, will pick up the format string and display the data as you requested.* ❦

The second issue is that some of the time periods show a value of 0.00%; for example, the year 1997, and the first quarter and first month of that year. This is because the FoodMart corporation began selling in 1997 so there are no figures for the preceding period and therefore no comparison can be made. The total for 1998 is also zero, and that's because the value for the previous period (the 1997 total) is itself zero.

The good news is that the expression is working but from a business angle the news is far from good. Look at the figures from 1998.

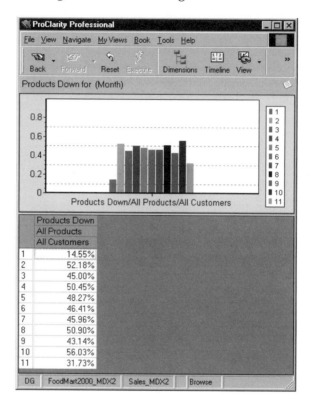

We haven't included the December 1998 figures here because, as discussed, there are no sales figures for that month.

Sales fell for almost half of our products in this year.

Let's look at which products are affected.

Apparently drink sales fell the most at 60%. So let's drill down into drinks and find out more information.

Now we can see which category of drink contributes most: it's alcoholic beverages which fell by 62.5%.

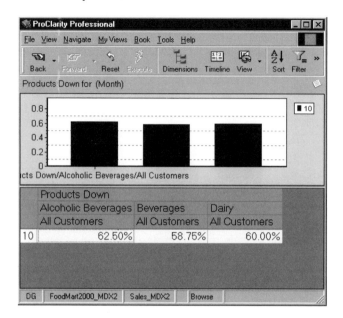

❝ *This is a powerful indication that we're working with sample data here – when did alcoholic beverages ever show falling sales in reality?* ❞

Building the Products Down calculated member has given us a whole new perspective on our data. OK, it may be nonsensical data in this instance but you get the idea. We've just demonstrated how, by using this relatively simple calculated member, we can start performing some very powerful analysis. We can go even further and drill down to find exactly which products sell least well and then try to analyze by some other dimension to find out why this might be so.

Summary

Those are the business benefits but what about our progress with the MDX language?

Once again we used the Descendants function: this, as you know by now, is an extremely powerful and versatile function. In this case we use it to ensure that a function works at a specific level. Often this will be the lowest level of a hierarchy, as in our example, but this is not necessarily so.

It is also worth pointing out again that it's easiest to construct these complex expressions one piece at a time. It would be a very difficult task to start with the original problem statement and try to write a complete expression. The best way to go about it is to break the whole big problem up into little problems, to find the small expressions that solve the little problems and then put those all together.

Lastly we saw how you can use the `Filter` function to narrow down a large set to just a subset that contains the data that interests you.

Function	Requires	Returns
Filter	Set, condition	Set

Chapter 10

Setting the default member

Resources:

Starting database – FoodMart2000_MDX2
Cube – Sales_MDX2
Completed sample database – FoodMart2000_EndChap11
MDX samples – CHAP10.TXT

Up to this point we have written expressions that only reference one, two or maybe three dimensions. Behind the scenes MDX is actually generating an expression that applies to all the dimensions. In the background the system takes the default member of each dimension and appends it onto the expression. The default member for a dimension is usually at the All level, and the All level typically has only one member – All. So for the Product dimension the default member is All Products; you could say that All Products is the default default member.

So dimensions have default members: why should this concern us as it appears not to have had any impact on our use of MDX thus far? While it's true that it doesn't necessarily affect database administrators (DBAs) who prepare cubes for use by others, those others – the business users whose requirements we are servicing – may take a rather different view.

Take the FoodMart Corporation's cube, for instance. The Time dimension doesn't have an All level; Year is the highest level in the Time dimension. The default member, therefore, will be the first member at the Year level, which is 1997. In the screen shot below the Cube Editor (at the top of the screen when you are using the data tab) is showing the default members for the Product, Store and Time dimensions: they are All Products, All Stores and 1997 respectively.

Product	All Products	▼
Store	All Stores	▼
Time	1997	▼

So what's wrong with year 1997 being the default member? Firstly it's several years ago and so the data isn't at all up-to-date, and secondly it's not the most recent year for which we have data. Users working with the cube are most likely to want to start with the most recent data and they won't be happy with having to navigate to the current period every time. This particular default member is quite likely to been seen as a problem by business users, though discontent will be expressed in different terms; perhaps "Why does it always show me those ancient figures? Doesn't it know we're in 2002?"

In our sample cube the most recent year is 1998, so we can just make that the default member for the Time dimension. That'll fix it... won't it? Well, yes, but only for twelve months. If you take this approach, every year you'll have to change the default member manually for every cube with a Time dimension. This is not at all an elegant solution: there must be something better we can do.

Indeed there is. We can set the default member of the Time dimension to act dynamically so that it will, in effect, be able to identify the current year and present that data to the user as the default.

Defining a custom default member

We've already met the function that will be of great help here; it's the LastSibling function introduced in Chapter 6 which looks at all the siblings of a member and returns the last one.

❻ *The way LastSibling works implies that the members in a dimension are ordered somehow. For now, it is safe to assume it's normal to have years sorted from the most recent back to the furthest away in time. In Chapter 14 we show you how to set up custom orders if you want to alter the default.*

Typically, Siblings are defined as members with the same parent. What about members that don't have a parent, as is the case at the highest level in a dimension, and as is true for the members at our Year level? As you might expect, Siblings is simply taken to refer to all the members at that level. ❾

We can pick an existing member of the year dimension, say, 1997, and apply the LastSibling function to it so it will return the most recent year.

Here we'll need to edit a dimension for the first time, so we won't be using the Cube Editor. Instead, we need the Dimension Editor. In the Tree view of the cube in Analysis Manager, expand the view of Shared Dimensions.

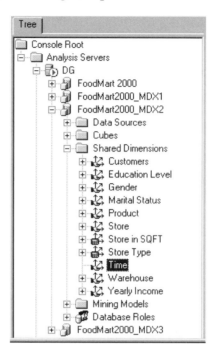

Right click on the Time dimension and select Edit.... In the Dimension Editor, click on the Advanced properties tab and highlight the Default Member property.

Click on the ellipsis button and in the Set Default Member dialog you can see that there is presently no custom default member setting for the Time dimension.

From here you can pick any of the members in the Time dimension to be the default member, and it can be any member at any level. Members with children at lower levels can be expanded and collapsed with a click in the usual way. Alternatively you can write an MDX expression to specify the default member, and as this is a book all about MDX, we'll do the MDX thing.

You can type the MDX expression directly into the slot in the dialog, which is easy with a brief expression like this one, or you can click on the ellipsis button to open the MDX Builder for building more complex expressions. We'll just type:

```
[1997].LastSibling
```

This expression takes the year 1997 and finds its last sibling which in our data-starved cube will be 1998, but if we added data for another five years, the expression would point to 2003.

Save the change to the dimension, and browsing the cube with the Cube Editor, we can see that the default member for Time is now 1998.

Product	All Products	▼
Store	All Stores	▼
Time	1998	▼

So now users will always be able to see the most recent data when they start work with our cube and the DBA can relax knowing that the problem has been fixed for keeps with a dynamic solution.

Defining a different custom default member

Unfortunately, DBAs can rarely relax for long: here's another problem brought to you by a cube user near you. "It's great that I can see data from the most recent year, but why do I then have to filter to look at the current month? I want to see the current month's data as soon as I start."

It appears the default member needs another tweak. This calls for the LastChild function which returns the last child of a given member. We want the last month, which can also be described as the last child of the last quarter.

Go to the Dimension Editor again and edit the default member. The start of our expression is fine – we still want it to find the last sibling of 1997. But now we also want to find the last child of this last sibling (which will be the last member at the Quarter level), and the last child of last quarter (which will be the last member at the Month level). So we can write:

```
[Time].[1997].LastSibling.LastChild.LastChild
```

Save the dimension and browse the cube. The default member for Time has certainly changed: it now says 12 instead of 1998. Excellent. Click on the down arrow button to the far right of the Time dimension display and you'll see this tree view.

Time	12	▼

```
⊞ ● 1997
⊟ ● 1998
    ⊞ ● Q1
    ⊞ ● Q2
    ⊞ ● Q3
    ⊟ ● Q4
          ● 10
          ● 11
          ● 12
```

However, when you look at the data display...

	MeasuresLevel	
+ Country	Unit Sales	Sales
All Customers		
+ Canada		
+ Mexico		
+ USA		

it doesn't look so good. There is no data. The new default member assumes that data is present for every month in the Time dimension but in our sample cube, there is no data for December 1998. In fact, if the Time dimension was defined to accept data up until 2003, our default member would happily open up in 2003 regardless of the fact that the last available data is for November 1998. Basically, it's not working at all well.

❻ *You may also have wondered, having read about elegance in MDX code, about the ungainly appearance of an expression ending* LastSibling.LastChild. LastChild. *If so, your wonderings have proved well placed; we can do better than this.* ❾

How do we fix things so that the cube opens at the last month that has data associated with it? We need an even more dynamic default member that in some way identifies the last month that contains data. This is quite a common business problem, especially for inventory and other retail systems.

Defining a fully dynamic custom default member

We'll demonstrate one approach to solving this problem using the Filter function and a new function called IsEmpty. The IsEmpty function performs a very simple task: it takes an expression and will return either minus one or zero, depending on whether the expression will evaluate to an empty cell or not.

❻ *The* IsEmpty *function is essentially answering the question "Is this cell empty?" in Boolean logic. It can only ever give one of two answers: either minus one which equates to true (i.e. the cell is empty) or zero which equates to false (no, the cell is not empty, it has content).* ❾

We want to look at all the months, filter out all those that are not empty and then pick up the last not-empty one. We start with the Filter function and the set we want it to work upon is a set of all months. Finding all the months is easy: we go to the Month level and use the Members function to return all months:

```
Filter([Time].[Month].Members,...)
```

The Filter function now needs a condition to evaluate so it can return a subset of all months. We want to identify the months with data using the IsEmpty function, but we want to flip IsEmpty round so it returns not the ones that are empty but the ones that have data in them. This we do by putting NOT in front of it, like this:

```
Filter([Time].[Month].Members, NOT IsEmpty...)
```

Lastly, we want to point NOT IsEmpty at the current time period.

```
Filter( [Time].[Month].Members,
NOT IsEmpty(Time.CurrentMember))
```

This is the completed Filter function which identifies all the months with data. Now we want to pick out the last one so we can use it as our default member. This is where we use the Tail function again, an old friend from Chapter 7. We want the last element of the set:

```
Tail(Filter( [Time].[Month].Members,
NOT IsEmpty(Time.CurrentMember)), 1)
```

We're almost there. But, once again, Tail is going to return a set and we're going to need a member. So, once again, we'll use the Item function to resolve the potential mismatch and extract the member from the set (as covered in Chapter 7).

```
Tail(Filter( [Time].[Month].Members,
NOT IsEmpty(Time.CurrentMember)),1).Item(0)
```

This is the complete expression that will identify the last month with data for use as our custom default member.

Now we know what to write, return to the Dimension Editor and enter the expression as the default member (this is where the MDX Builder comes into its own). Save the dimension and browse the cube. Miraculously, the default member for the Time dimension has changed again, this time to month 11 in 1998:

Product	All Products	▼
Store	All Stores	▼
Time	11	▼

	MeasuresLevel	
+ Country	Unit Sales	Sales
All Customers	53,807.00	$113,787.84
+ Canada	4,827.00	$10,265.37
+ Mexico	17,912.00	$37,462.18
+ USA	31,068.00	$66,060.29

Schema Data

which, as we know, is the last month with any data.

| Time | 11 | ▼ |

- ⊞ ● 1997
- ⊟ ● 1998
  - ⊞ ● Q1
  - ⊞ ● Q2
  - ⊞ ● Q3
  - ⊟ ● Q4
    - ● 10
    - ● 11
    - ● 12

Default measures

Incidentally, you can also set a default measure for a cube. This is one of the basic properties for a cube and it identifies the measure to be returned by an expression if no measure is specified by that expression. It is not obligatory to set a default measure; if you don't, expressions that don't define a measure will still work, they'll just return an arbitrary measure.

Summary

It's all taken a long time to explain, but you've been learning hard all the while and another new function, IsEmpty, has been introduced. It can be used as it stands or with its behavior flipped by adding NOT.

Equally importantly, you've seen how something that starts out as a static setting, such as the default member, can be made so dynamic that it can change automatically as alterations are made to a dimension. Both time periods and data can be added to the cube and the dynamic MDX expression just takes it all in its stride.

Finally, the method of building expressions incrementally has again proved its worth.

Function	Requires	Returns
LastSibling	Member	Member
LastChild	Member	Member
Filter	Set, condition	Set
IsEmpty	Expression	Boolean
Members	Level or Dimension	Set
Tail	Set, count	Set

Chapter 11

Member properties and dimension security

Resources:

Starting database – FoodMart2000_MDX2
Cube – Sales_MDX2
Completed sample database – FoodMart2000_EndChap11
MDX samples – CHAP11.TXT

Member properties

You may recall that we touched briefly upon member properties back in Chapter 1. Now we're going to take a further look at them and see how the value of these properties can be maximized using MDX.

A member property is an additional piece of information about a particular member that is relevant only to that member. In a Customer dimension, for instance, customers might have properties that tell us, say, their address and email address. In the Store dimension, each store might have properties to indicate how many parking spaces it has to offer its customers, the name of the current manager, the type of store and/or, to quote the example from Chapter 1, the size of the store.

Member properties are often used to store the information that will be useful for analysis in a cube but which wouldn't make a very sensible dimension – it's hard to imagine what value a 'customer parking' dimension might bring to a cube. However, just because data doesn't sit well in a dimension doesn't mean it can't be useful. The information that we are able to hold as the property of a member can be immensely valuable and can be used to improve analyses and inform business decisions.

How can you find out if a member has any properties associated with it? In the tree view that's shown to the top left of the Cube Editor, expand the Store dimension to see the levels in the hierarchy and expand the Store Name level. You'll see a folder called Member properties and if you expand that,

you'll see that members at the Store Name level have three properties: Store Manager, Store Sqft (square feet) and Store Type. This view doesn't, of course, tell us whether there is any data for any of the properties for any of the stores. To find that out, we need a new MDX function.

It's the Properties function and its role is to let you query member properties. Simple to use, all you need to know is the name of the member and of the property that interests you: the member name is placed in front of the Properties function and the property name comes afterwards, like this:

```
Store.CurrentMember.Properties("Store Manager")
```

❝ *The Properties function always returns a string so keep this in mind as we proceed.* ❞

This expression will return the name of the manager for the current store. So, if you use it to create a calculated measure called, say, Store Mgr, then this MDX query:

```
SELECT
{ [Time].[1998] } ON COLUMNS ,
{ Descendants([Store].[All Stores].[USA],3) } ON ROWS
FROM [Sales_MDX2]
WHERE ( [Measures].[Store Mgr] )
```

will show you the managers of all the stores in the USA.

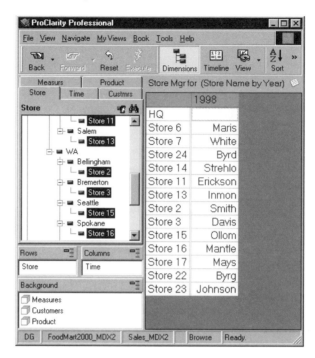

So we can see that the manager of the Salem store is Inmon. Whether this is **the** Inmon (as in 'Bill', the 'father of data warehousing') or just any old Inmon isn't clear but since this is only sample data we don't really care.

What we do care about is using member properties to solve real business problems. So we'll introduce another business scenario, one in which our company sells data about different stores. In this scenario the stores may well not belong to our company, we are just in the business of selling data about stores. We have a scheme for attracting buyers of our data which is to give away the data about small stores as a kind of loss leader to hook in customers. If customers decide they want data about the larger stores, then we'll start charging them.

Dimension security

This scenario is also a good opportunity to bring in another of MDX's useful features, that of dimension security. In order to describe dimension security, we'll start with a brief and simple overview of the way in which

Analysis Services lets you control the ways users can access databases and cubes.

Analysis Services employs roles (database roles and cube roles) in order to control access to databases. A role is a convenient way of controlling what actions a user can perform within the database: when a role is defined, various permissions can be granted which allow a user read-only access, for instance, or read/write access.

Once a database role has been defined, users can be allocated to it and each user will automatically be granted the permissions specified in the role. The database role can also be allocated to any cube in the database. The allocation process will create a cube role with the same set of permissions as the original database role. The cube role can then be tweaked to include any extra permissions (or to remove existing permissions) for the cube. A cube role applies to a single cube.

The default in a cube role is to allow all members to see all dimension members in a cube. One of the more advanced examples of cube role tweaking is to restrict access to dimensions and this brings us to our current topic, dimension security. We'll cover more of the whys and wherefores as we solve our new business problem.

Using member properties and dimension security

In order for our loss leader scheme to work, we need to be able to restrict access to data in the stores dimension; in other words, to define the dimension security for the stores dimension so that we can give two sorts of access. One will be unrestricted access to the data on small stores and one will grant access to data on the larger stores but this will only be made available to paying customers.

Let's take a quick look at the stores we have in Washington and Oregon so that later on it will be easy to see whether our solution is working:

- USA	- OR	OR Total
		+ Portland
		+ Salem
	- WA	WA Total
		+ Bellingham
		+ Bremerton
		+ Seattle
		+ Spokane
		+ Tacoma
		+ Walla Walla
		+ Yakima

There is only one store per city, so there are two stores in Oregon and seven in Washington.

For our purposes, we define the size of a store by its square footage, so stores which are less than 21,000 sq ft are considered to be small. The square footage of each store is held in the `Store Sqft` member property of `Store Name`.

OK, as always, we need a game plan for solving this problem. We need to find all stores, find the square footage of each and filter out those stores with a square footage of less than 21,000 sq ft.

As before, we use the `Member` function to find all stores:

```
[Store].[Store Name].Members
```

and then we want to query each member to find the value in its `Store Sqft` property using the `Properties` function:

```
Store.CurrentMember.Properties("Store Sqft")
```

The `Properties` function, you'll recall, always returns a string which isn't good news here. We want to be able to compare the square footage values for each store in order to find the small ones. To do this, we need to convert the strings to numerical values and to perform the conversion we can use the VBA function called `Val`.

❝ *"Wait a minute," you cry. "Isn't this a book about MDX? How did Visual Basic for Applications sneak in?" MDX has many useful tricks up its sleeve and one is its ability to use a VBA function just as if it was an MDX function. In fact, Analysis Services can automatically make use of many VBA and Excel functions so even though they're not part of Analysis Services you can use them seamlessly in your MDX code.* ❞

The `Val` function returns the numbers contained in a string as a numeric value. The string to be converted is wrapped up in braces and placed after the function: in our case, the string is returned by the `Properties` function so we'd write:

```
Val(Store.CurrentMember.Properties("Store Sqft"))
```

The code to find all members at the `Store Name` level goes in front:

```
Store.[Store Name].Members,
Val(Store.CurrentMember.Properties("Store Sqft"))
```

and now we're ready to add a Filter function to give us only those stores where the square footage is less than 21,000, like this:

```
Filter(Store.[Store Name].Members,
Val(Store.CurrentMember.Properties("Store Sqft")) < 21000)
```

and that's the expression complete.

So now we can identify the stores about which we will supply free data and those for which we want to charge. That's half the solution, but we still need to be able to restrict access to data on that basis, so we'll put our expression on hold for the moment.

In order to implement this, we need to delve into the security settings and create a role. This database contains only one cube so it doesn't really matter if we create a database or cube role, so we'll choose to create a cube role. Analysis Manager contains yet another editor for managing security and to reach it, right click on the cube and select Manage Roles.

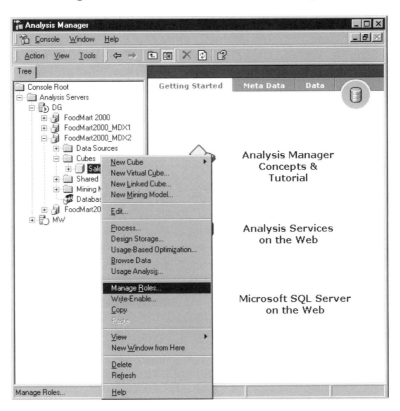

The Cube Role Manager shows all roles that are associated with the cube.

You can see a role called All Users and its membership is Everyone. This means that absolutely everyone coming in from the far corners of the internet can work under this role, so this is the role in which we want to introduce the new restriction on access to the store dimension.

With the All Users role highlighted, click the Edit button and then the Dimensions tab. Click in the cell that shows the Rule in place for the Store dimension (at present it's Unrestricted) and then pop down the list of options. Choose Custom.

Now either click on the ellipsis button that will have appeared under Custom Settings (it only appears when Custom is selected under Rule)

Name	Permission	Rule	Custom Settings
Measures	Read	Unrestricted	
Store	Read	Custom	...
Time	Read	Unrestricted	
Customers	Read	Unrestricted	
Product	Read	Unrestricted	

Summary | Membership | Dimensions | Cells | Options

Set security parameters for a dimension's read and write permissions.

Dimensions:

or double click anywhere in the Store/Custom Settings cell and the Custom Dimension Security dialog opens up: click on the Advanced tab.

Custom Dimension Security: Store

Permission: Read

Description:

Basic Advanced Common

Type MDX statements in the boxes or click "...".

Top Level: [Store].[(All)]

Bottom Level: [Store].[Store Name]

Note: Bottom level for Read and Read/Write must be consistent. Changes here will affect the setting for Read/Write.

Allowed Members:

Denied Members:

Restore Defaults...   OK   Cancel   Help

Faced with this screen, now seems like a good time for some more information about how dimension security can be set up. There are basically two approaches to defining security depending on whether you are optimistic or pessimistic. The pessimistic approach is to deny access to everything in the dimension except to a specific set of members, referred to as allowed members. The optimistic approach is to grant access to everything except for that set of members, now known as denied members.

One important difference between these approaches is the effect they have during an incremental update to a dimension.

❝ *Analysis Services permits the incremental updating of dimensions when the cube is processed. This can be very useful when rows have been added to any of the cube's dimension tables since the cube was last processed.* ❞

If you take the optimistic view and allow everything except for specific members, when you run an incremental update of the dimension, it will be possible for new members to be added. Should a new store be opened, for instance, it can be added to the dimension during the update. If, on the other hand, you react pessimistically and deny everything except for specific members, it will not be possible to add new members during an incremental update.

This time we'll do the pessimistic thing and deny access to everything except the allowed members. Start by entering a description in the space at the top of the dialog box for the customized permission, something along the lines of Small Stores. Now click on the ellipsis button to the right of the Allowed Members: box to open the MDX Builder and enter the expression we built a short while ago – here it is again:

```
Filter(Store.[Store Name].Members,
Val(Store.CurrentMember.Properties("Store Sqft")) < 21000)
```

![MDX Builder dialog box showing the MDX expression "Filter([Store].[Store Name].Members, Val (Store.CurrentMember.Properties("Store Sqft")) < 21000)" with Data tree listing Store hierarchy and Functions list]

and click OK to paste it into the Allowed Members box. Click OK again and the new custom setting is now displayed in the Cube Role editor.

❺ *If you write expressions in a text editor it's worth noting that the MDX editor is very picky about its inverted commas. If you write your MDX in Microsoft Word, for example, and use the curly double open and close inverted commas, and copy and paste the expression into the editor, you'll find it won't work. The commas are replaced by blocks and a syntax error is reported. Using the straight double inverted commas from the Insert, Symbol utility in Word cures this glitch, or you can simply edit the expression once it has been pasted into the expression editor.* ❺

Dimensions:

Name	Permission	Rule	Custom Settings
Measures	Read	Unrestricted	
Store	Read	Custom	Small Stores
Time	Read	Unrestricted	
Customers	Read	Unrestricted	
Product	Read	Unrestricted	

Click OK again, and back in the Cube Role Manager, the Store dimension is now shown in the list of restricted dimensions.

We seem to have done it, but we have a potential problem with testing the newly edited role. It's highly likely that you are an administrator with all the rights and privileges of data access entailed by that position: you will be able to see everything everywhere. So do you have to log off, create a new user and log on again in order to adopt a different persona, one where you're an underprivileged user rather than an all-powerful administrator? In situations like this in the past, that was indeed the only solution, and it was as tedious and as time-consuming as you would expect.

Happily, Analysis Manager has a new feature which enables you to test roles without all the hassle. Choose a role and it will mimic the security permissions for that role so that you can see and do exactly what a user allocated to that role can see and do.

One of the buttons along the bottom of the Cube Role Manager screen is one called Test Role (it's shown in the screen shot above). Highlight the role you want to test, click the button and there you are in the Cube Browser, inspecting data as a member of the All Users role.

Let's check out whether our MDX expression is working by dragging the Store dimension onto the grid and expanding the list of stores in Washington and Oregon.

- OR	OR Total	60,612.00
	+ Portland	25,266.00
	WA Total	126,287.00
- WA	+ Walla Walla	2,244.00
	+ Yakima	9,710.00

Instead of seven towns in Washington, only two are now visible: Yakima and Walla Walla. This seems reasonable as they are smaller towns well away from the more populous west coast. Oregon is down to one store instead of two. But the one that we can see is in Portland: though not the state capital, Portland is still a large city and it's surprising that this store is being filtered out because it is small. Perhaps our expression isn't working as we'd planned.

Close the Cube Browser and the Cube Role Manager. This gets you back to Analysis Manager and it also means that you will have your administrator rights restored to you.

Edit the cube, browse the data and expand the information about the Portland store until you can see Store 11 member. Right click on it, select Member Properties and these are displayed.

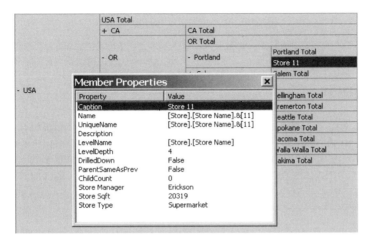

A-ha! So the Portland store is a borderline case with 20,319 square feet of space which puts it a mere 681 square feet short of our 21,000 cut-off point.

Everything seems to be OK, but let's look at Walla Walla's square footage (Store 22) just to make sure.

Oh. So that's why Walla Walla shows up – there is no value for the store area. Our sample data isn't as comprehensive as perhaps it should be. In fact, there is no value for Yakima or any of the other stores we can see in the restricted set.

❻ *It's easy to develop complete faith in the answers that analyses present to you, but these answers can only ever reflect the accuracy of the data in the database and the accuracy of the manipulations. Once data becomes complex, anomalies like these are almost bound to occur and it can be useful to go back to the original data now and again just to check that you and your expressions aren't making any unsupportable assumptions.* ❾

Summary

In solving this business problem, we've taken several further steps up the learning curve which is, hopefully, beginning to flatten out. We've looked at member properties and seen how they can be queried with the Properties function. Using member properties as a filter criteria can be a useful way of looking at your data, allowing you to segment the data depending on the property.

We've demonstrated the use of external VBA functions: these and a range of Excel functions can be accessed completely seamlessly within MDX. You don't have to think twice about using them, you just do it.

Lastly we've looked briefly at dimension security, showing how MDX can be used to define extremely dynamic dimension security and how member properties can be used as criteria for defining that dimension security.

Function	Requires	Returns
Properties	Member name	String
Val *(VBA function)*	String	Value

Chapter 12

Distinct Count

Resources:

Starting database – FoodMart2000_MDX3
Cube – Sales
Completed sample database – FoodMart2000_EndChap14

Many times in business situations we want to know exactly how many somethings we have; the somethings may be customers, for instance, or products. It's a straightforward enough question to a human being and you might expect the answer to be simply found too, but in the past it has proved surprisingly troublesome. All that's behind us now as MDX has a splendidly useful Distinct Count function.

It's time for another scenario: you're managing a cube for a large computer retailing business and the sales manager has just asked "How many customers do I have?" Below is a simple table showing a Products dimension grouped by hardware and software, with two measures, the sales and the number of customers.

	Sales	No of customers
All products	$80,000	200
Hardware	$33,000	80
Computers	$20,000	70
Monitors	$8,000	60
Printers	$5,000	30
Software	$47,000	150
Home	$15,000	100
Business	$25,000	100
Games	$7,000	80

We sum all values for sales so the total for all products is $80,000. Fine, but what we really want to know is how many customers we have, that is, how many customers contributed to the sales total. So we look at the number of customers shown against all products and see that we have 200 customers. What does that mean exactly? Look at the numbers of customers buying the three categories of software and we have eighty customers buying games, a hundred buying business software and a hundred buying home software. However, the total number of customers against software sales is 150, not 280. Isn't this an anomaly? The correct answer is 'no' because the same customer may buy games and home applications, and possibly business applications as well. So this set of figures is correct; the problem is that if we build a cube from the underlying data, unless we tell it to behave differently, it will simply sum the customers in the same way as the Sales values.

In fact we often wish to avoid counting any customer more than once because doing so produces all sorts of misleading values, not only of the number of customers but also values such as the average amount spent per customer, the number of brochures to print for a customer mail-shot and any possible correlations between purchases by a single customer that could be exploited to make additional sales. The Distinct Count function allows you to do all of this, and more, in your cube.

Distinct Count is an unusual function because it can only be used by a measure. It's used in measures to produce an aggregated value and it does this by aggregating all instances of the same entity in order to ascertain the number of unique values. Despite this atypical feature, Distinct Count is very simple to use.

The cube we'll use is the Sales cube from the FoodMart2000_MDX3 database. We want to build a measure that will tell us how many individual customers we have, so open the Cube Editor and create a new measure. From the Schema, click on the column in the fact table that identifies the entities you want to count, drag it over to the Measures folder and drop it. We want the customer_id column so drag it across and a new measure of the same name appears. (Alternatively you could right click on Measures in the Tree view and select New Measure... and select customer_id as the source column and click OK).

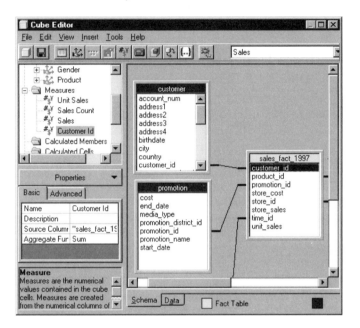

In the Basic properties tab, change the Name to reflect the new measure's role in life – Customer Count sounds good – and then double click on the cell in the properties list that show the current Aggregate Function to be Sum. From the list, choose Distinct Count.

❡ *The complete list of Aggregate Functions supported in MDX is Sum, Count, Max, Min and* Distinct Count: *as the names suggest, all of these functions perform an aggregation of some sort.*

Aggregate function	Returned value
Sum	The sum of the input values
Min	The lowest of the input values
Max	The highest of the input values
Count	The number of input values
Distinct Count	The number of unique input values

If you move to the Data view, you'll see a message that says you'll only be able to see sample data until the cube is processed. Save the cube, click Tools and select Process to process the cube.

Processing the sample cube will take longer because data from the relational source is used to calculate the distinct count as an additional and separate step in the processing run. The good news is that you only pay that price once and with the cube processed, querying the Customer Count measure will be very fast.

Here we can see the customer count for all customers and for a range of customer subsets. The new measure is also shown with its basic properties.

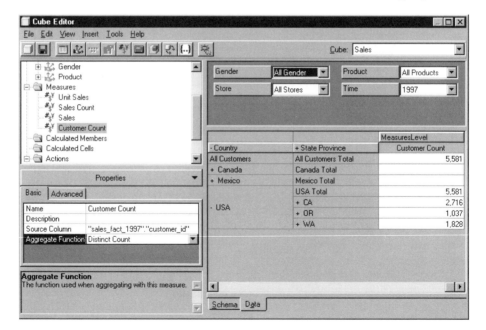

This brief chapter will, we hope, bring joy to anyone who has struggled with distinct counting in the past.

Chapter 13

Parent–Child dimensions

Resources:

    Starting database – FoodMart2000_MDX3
    Cube – Budget
    Completed sample database – FoodMart2000_EndChap14

In Chapter 14 we will be looking at a variety of features that are best demonstrated using a Parent–Child dimension. The good news is that these dimensions are easy to understand, the bad is that Chapter 14 makes no sense at all unless you are familiar with them. Of course, in your OLAP travels you may already have become intimately acquainted with this type of dimension, in which case please feel free to skip this and dive immediately into Chapter 14.

Since you're still reading...

Parent–Child dimensions are best described by contrasting them with 'normal' dimensions. A typical dimension table for a star schema might look something like this:

Day_id	Day	Month	Quarter	Year
367	01/01/1997	January	Q1	1997
368	02/01/1997	January	Q1	1997
...	...	...	...	...
397	31/01/1997	January	Q1	1997
398	01/02/1997	February	Q1	1997
...	...	...	...	...
456	31/03/1997	March	Q1	1997
457	01/04/1997	April	Q2	1997
458	02/04/1997	April	Q2	1997
and	so	on		

Here we are storing information about each day and we are also storing hierarchical information about how days build up into months, quarters and years. So we have four levels and multiple members at each level. However, note that we aren't storing information specifically about any of the members apart from the days. There is one row in the table for each specified day, but no rows for any months, quarters etc. Instead, each of the higher levels (Year, Quarter and Month) is represented by a column in the table. In the Month column, for example, we store the name of the member at the month level (e.g. February) to which any given day belongs.

Note that none of the month members (such as February) have a unique identifier in this dimension table. The implication of this is that February can't be referenced by an entry in the fact table, so the cube itself can only ever contain data about February that is derived from the 'daily' data. This, of course, isn't normally a problem because all the data for the higher levels is logically derivable from the base data by aggregation.

Now, suppose that you want to store information about another hierarchy, one that looks like this:

The fact table holds financial transactions and each transaction is one of eight types as defined by the leaf members – Cost of Goods Sold, Gross Sales and so on down to Marketing. The first four are aggregated up to produce Net Sales and the last four to give Total Expense. In turn these two are aggregated to give Net Income.

No problem, we simply use a dimension table like this.

Account_id	Account_description	Level 2	Level 1	Account_type
3200	Cost of Goods Sold	Net Sales	Net Income	Income
3100	Gross Sales	Net Sales	Net Income	Income
3500	Return	Net Sales	Net Income	Expense
3300	Tax Refunds	Net Sales	Net Income	Income
4100	General & Administration	Total Expense	Net Income	Expense
4200	Information Systems	Total Expense	Net Income	Expense
4400	Lease	Total Expense	Net Income	Expense
4300	Marketing	Total Expense	Net Income	Expense

We are using two columns for the hierarchy information, Level 1 and Level 2, and another is used for storing additional information that the business users have specified – Account_type.

Now, suppose the hierarchy becomes more complex.

A transaction in the fact table can now be classified as one of ten types (Assets and Liabilities are now included) and both of these contribute directly to All Account. But our original design of the dimension table only allows facts in the fact table to point to members at the lowest level.

Well, this happens to be an unbalanced hierarchy, which means that not every account type is the same number of levels down from All level. Hmmm. Well, we could try to represent this information in a standard dimension table like this:

Account_id	Account_description	Level 3	Level 2	Level 1	Account_type
1000	Assets			All	Asset
2000	Liabilities			All	Liability
5000	Net Income			All	Income
3000	Net Sales		Net Income	All	Income
3200	Cost of Goods Sold	Net Sales	Net Income	All	Income
3100	Gross Sales	Net Sales	Net Income	All	Income
3500	Return	Net Sales	Net Income	All	Expense
3300	Tax Refunds	Net Sales	Net Income	All	Income
4000	Total Expense		Net Income	All	Expense
4100	General & Administration	Total Expense	Net Income	All	Expense
4200	Information Systems	Total Expense	Net Income	All	Expense
4400	Lease	Total Expense	Net Income	All	Expense
4300	Marketing	Total Expense	Net Income	All	Expense

or we could try it like this:

Account_id	Account_description	Parent	GrandParent	GGrandParent	Account_type
1000	Assets	All			Asset
2000	Liabilities	All			Liability
5000	Net Income	All			Income
3000	Net Sales	Net Income	All		Income
3200	Cost of Goods Sold	Net Sales	Net Income	All	Income
3100	Gross Sales	Net Sales	Net Income	All	Income
3500	Return	Net Sales	Net Income	All	Expense
3300	Tax Refunds	Net Sales	Net Income	All	Income
4000	Total Expense	Net Income	All		Expense
4100	General & Administration	Total Expense	Net Income	All	Expense
4200	Information Systems	Total Expense	Net Income	All	Expense
4400	Lease	Total Expense	Net Income	All	Expense
4300	Marketing	Total Expense	Net Income	All	Expense

Now each one has a unique identifier and so each can be referenced by the fact table. However, this will become rather messy if (as often happens in reality) we end up with a large number of members at many different levels. Can we be a little more imaginative about how we structure this table? Answer: "No, we are going to just have to put up with this."

OK, just kidding. We can swap to a model where we have a row for every member in the hierarchy, irrespective of the level at which they occur. We can also dump all of the explicit level columns from the table; in their place we put a single column which points to the parent of the member – like this:

Account_id	Account_parent	Account_description	Account_type
1000		Assets	Asset
2000		Liabilities	Liability
3000	5000	Net Sales	Income
3100	3000	Gross Sales	Income
3200	3000	Cost of Goods Sold	Income
3300	3000	Tax Refunds	Income
3500	3000	Return	Expense
4000	5000	Total Expense	Expense
4100	4000	General & Administration	Expense
4200	4000	Information Systems	Expense
4300	4000	Marketing	Expense
4400	4000	Lease	Expense
5000		Net Income	Income

❝ *Account_parent is a foreign key to the primary key – Account_id – and uses a self-join.* ❞

If you are prepared to take the time to follow all of the joins, you should discover that you can create the hierarchy above from this table. This is called a Parent–Child dimension because the table stores information about both parents and children in the same table. There is one row in the table for each and every member in the hierarchy. That row also contains a pointer to the parent of the member. It turns out that this way of describing a dimension happens to have other major advantages. As you will have guessed, these advantages are discussed as part of the next chapter.

Chapter 14

Advanced data modeling – Custom Order, Custom Rollup, Custom Members

Resources:

Starting database – FoodMart2000_MDX3
Cube – Budget
Completed sample database – FoodMart2000_EndChap14
MDX samples – CHAP14.TXT

The topics covered in this and the next chapter all come under the general heading of issues which typically need to be addressed in a financial application, so that is how we've illustrated them. However, once again, we want to stress that this is simply a convenient way of illustrating them – the topics can be applied in a host of different applications.

Usually we try to structure the data in a cube to reflect the way it is used in the real world. For cube users to make the most effective use of the data, they need to see 'their' data in ways that make sense to them so that they can analyze and manipulate it with confidence and without having to learn any special cubist approaches.

For this we'll use the Budget cube from FoodMart2000_MDX3 and in this cube we have four dimensions: Store and Time are just as before, and there is a Category dimension that holds values such as actual, budget, budget variance, forecast and so on. The fourth dimension is Account and this will hold the data such as sales, costs, maybe expenses – all the financial accounting stuff that's needed to present the data in the required way. Let's look at it with the Cube Editor:

The good news is that it's undeniably a cube, but the bad news is that it's not what's required by the users at all. Firstly, there's the question of ordering in the Category dimension. The category descriptions need to be displayed in an order that makes sense to a business user, rather than in the alphabetical order they're shown at present. So values for actuals should be followed by those for budget, then by any adjustments and finally by the forecast.

The second problem is rather more serious. The company's net income for 1997 is just over $189,000 which looks great (1998 looks even better!) – until we see how that total is being derived.

| Store | All Stores | ▼ |
| Time | 1997 | ▼ |

			MeasuresLevel	▲
Category Description	- Level 02	+ Level 03	Amount	
	Assets			
	Liabilities			
Current Year's Actuals		Net Income Total	$189,345.56	
	- Net Income	+ Net Sales	$22,863.12	
		+ Total Expense	$166,482.44	
Current Year's Budget	All Account	All Account Total		▼

Schema | Data

It looks suspiciously like the company's expenses of $166,000-odd are being added to the net sales figure to derive the net income. In other words, the figures in our current cube are a gross misrepresentation of the company's performance. Back in Chapter 7 we talked about the default behavior of a cube which is to sum all values. This is again the crux of our problem: the values are being added and that is giving us the wrong answers.

Finally, one of the main reasons for building the cube was to do some budgeting, but there are no budget figures in the cube to support this. So, getting some budget figures into the cube is also a high priority. OK, let's get fixing these three problems.

Problem 1: Custom Order – ordering of members in a hierarchy

The members in a dimension are sorted by default into alphabetical order. While finding the city you want is easy in an alphabetical list, it's not the ideal way of presenting the categories in our Category dimension. What we need here is some custom sorting of the members.

Levels within a dimension have an advanced property called Order By that allows you, as the name suggests, to order the members within that level. We can see this using the dimension editor:

In this case the members are being ordered by the Name. OK, no problem, all we need to do is to find out to what 'Name' in this context refers. The answer lies in the Basic properties.

❝ *The first property in the list is Name and it is tempting to think that 'Order By – Name' is referring to this – tempting, but incorrect. This is simply the name of the level itself and it is logically unreasonable to try and order the members of a level by the name of the level.* ❞

The answer is that 'Order By – Name' is pointing to the property 'Member Name Column'.

OK, that has answered one question but it may, depending on how much you know about cube design, have simply introduced another – "So what's the difference between Member Key Column and Member Name Column?" We'll digress briefly from custom ordering to cover this difference for those who haven't come across it so far.

Member Key Column and Member Name Column

Both the Member Key Column and Member Name Column are pointing to columns in the dimension table (back in the source database which is an Access database called FoodMart 2000 Before Demos.mdb). Here is some sample data from that table:

	category_id	category_description
▶	ACTUAL	Current Year's Actuals
	ADJUSTMENT	Adjustment for Budget input
	BUDGET	Current Year's Budget
	FORECAST	Forecast

category : Table — Record: 1 of 4

and here is some from the fact table:

store_id	account_id	exp_date	time_id	category_id	amount
3	4400	01/04/1997	457	ACTUAL	$214.10
3	4400	01/05/1997	487	ACTUAL	$214.10
3	4400	01/06/1997	518	ACTUAL	$214.10
3	4400	01/07/1997	548	ACTUAL	$214.10
3	4400	01/08/1997	579	ACTUAL	$214.10
3	4400	01/09/1997	610	ACTUAL	$214.10

expense_fact : Table — Record: 1 of 3000

In the Cube Editor:

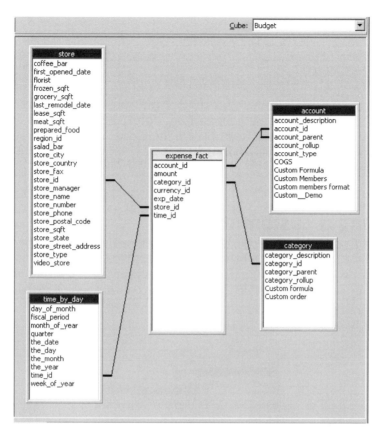

we can see that the member key column is pointing to `category_id` in the Category table which is the primary key of that table. So `category.category_id` is the column at the 'one' end of a one-to-many join. In other words the data in this column uniquely identifies the rows in the dimension table and hence uniquely identifies the members of the dimension.

The member name column points to `category_description`, which holds the actual name by which a dimension's members are known and these are the names that are shown in the data pane.

An important point that comes out of all this is that these member names do not have to be unique for each member of the dimension (in this case they are, but the structure of the table offers no guarantees on the point).

The member keys, on the other hand, are held in a column that is the primary key. By definition, they **have** to be unique, **are** unique and always **will be** unique. No question.

❛ *But please don't think that we are trying to stress that this difference is particularly important or anything.* ❜

Of course, all of this is under your control and you don't have to set it up as shown here. For example, depending upon the level, it is relatively common to use the same column for both the member keys and the member names (see the section called 'More about &' at the end of this chapter).

Creating a custom order

OK, back in Advanced Properties, we now know what Name means in the Order By property. It means that the members are being sorted alphabetically on the data found in the Member Name column which turns out to be the column called category_description. So, if we change the Order By property to Key:

Hide Member If	Never hidden
Visible	True
Order By	Name
Custom Rollup Formula	Name
Custom Members	Key
Custom Member Options	False

the order would change to actuals, adjustments, budget and forecast, but in practice we won't do that because that isn't what we want either. What we do want is to be able to sort these into our own custom order.

Tweaking the order manually is a possibility and it's acceptable for a dimension with four members; however, a dimension can have tens, hundreds or even thousands of members. Dealing with each one manually would be very time consuming so there is another way to control the order and that's to use a member property to define a custom order. So we need to create a new member property and then use that new property to order the members.

Firstly you need a column in the dimension table which will define the ordering for each member and, being thoughtful individuals, we've already provided such a column for experimentation. If you look at the schema view of the `Category` dimension table, you'll see a column called 'Custom order':

and this is the data source table (held in the Access database called `FoodMart 2000 Before Demos.mdb`) showing the same column:

category_id	category_description	Custom order
ACTUAL	Current Year's Actuals	1
ADJUSTMENT	Adjustment for Budget input	3
BUDGET	Current Year's Budget	2
FORECAST	Forecast	4

Record: I◄ ◄   1   ► ►I ►* of 4

One benefit of having the column in the dimension table is that it can be populated automatically from, for instance, a stored procedure. Another benefit is that it keeps everything about the dimension in the same place for easy maintenance.

The second step is to set up a new member property based on data from this Custom order column. Just as we did in Chapter 11, right click on the Member Property folder (it's beneath the Category Description in the hierarchy view), select New Member Property, click on the Custom Order column:

and then on OK. The property name will have transmogrified itself into `Customorder`, so edit it to be `Custom Order`.

Now look at the advanced properties of Category Description again and, when you click to see the options available for the Order By property, you'll see three of them:

Select the new member property, Custom Order, save and reprocess the dimension. Open the Cube Editor to look at the results – you'll be asked to reprocess the cube first – and check out the order of the categories.

Here the Category Descriptions are shown in exactly the correct order with the values for actuals followed by those for budget, then by adjustments and finally by the forecast. Great, that problem's sorted.

Practical summary

While telling you how to create a custom order we have also tried to explain what we were doing as we went along, with the result that it all seems to have taken a long time to accomplish the work. And this may give the impression that these improvements to the cube are difficult and time consuming to implement whereas, in fact, once you are used to doing them, they are simple. So, here is a practical summary of what we have just achieved to show that the work involved is minimal.

Problem 1: `Custom Order` – ordering of members in a hierarchy

The members in a dimension are sorted by default into alphabetical order. We want to sort in a custom order.

1 Create a column (`Custom Order`) in the dimension table (`Category`) which will define the ordering for each member. *(This is done for you.)*
2 Add the appropriate sort-order information as data in this column. *(This is done for you.)*
3 Set up a new member property based on data from this `Custom Order` column. To do this: edit the `Category` dimension using the Dimension Editor, right click on the Member Property folder (it's beneath the Category Description in the hierarchy view), select New Member Property, click on the Custom Order column and click OK.
4 Now look at the advanced properties of Category Description and find the Order By property. When you click to see the options available for the Order By property, you'll see three of them including Custom Order. Select it. Save and reprocess the dimension.
5 Reprocess the cube.

Problem 2: Custom Rollup – when the cube's default behavior doesn't do the right job

The problem is that our expenses have been rolled up and added to sales and while this may give us a great value for net income, it's simply wrong.

❛ *Very wrong. In practice people like accountants can get surprisingly tense about this kind of error, and you end up getting aggravation about your aggregations.* ❜

This is another place where we need to control the order, not of the way things are displayed this time, but the order in which the values are rolled up to give aggregated values and what exactly each step in the rolling up operation should be. In other words, we need to define a custom rollup.

The default behavior, as you know, is to aggregate from the lowest level, summing everything up to produce aggregated totals. In this case expenses are being added to net sales to give an erroneous profit figure. We want to sum to get a total for expenses and do the same to find the net sales, but then we want to subtract the expenses total from the net sales total in order to find out the true profit figure. At a finer grain of detail, not all sales are credits – returns and cost of goods sold are actually expenses – so we want to subtract these from the net sales total too.

The aggregation of members is controlled by the tongue-twisting Unary operator (try that when sales of alcoholic beverages have increased). These can be applied to members in our Account dimension to force them to do what we want. There are five unary operators: +, -, *, / and ~. The first four behave as you'd expect and the tilde means that you do not want the data to be rolled up or included in any total.

The tilde is useful for such things as assets and liabilities which don't necessarily need to be rolled up, and it's also handy if you want to do a 'what if' simulation. You might want to include a hypothetical value as well as a true value in the cube. Then you could assign a tilde to the true value to leave it out of the calculations and roll up the hypothetical value into your 'what if' analysis.

There are two further pieces of information that you'll need when working with unary operators. The first is that they have what's called a solve order – simply the order in which the arithmetical steps are carried out – and that is taken directly from the ordering of members. Basically, the process starts at the top of the dimension and works downwards.

❡ *It is possible to change the solve order: you'd create a new member property, set its Type property to Sequence and assign sequence numbers corresponding to the new solve order in its Source Column property. It's a very similar process to the one we've just illustrated for defining a sort order.* ❡

Secondly, unary operators can be stored in a separate column in the source database.

OK, so we want to assign unary operators to the members in the Account dimension, so start by browsing the members in that dimension with the Dimension Editor:

The members all look perfectly normal with no visual indication that there's anything special about them. They'll just sum up as usual.

The unary operator to be used for each member is stored in a column in the source database: the approach is very similar to that used for storing the custom order of members. It's a particularly efficient process, especially when dealing with large numbers of members. Again, we've already put a column in our Account dimension table to hold the details of our custom rollup; it's called account_rollup and this is it in the schema view:

(The join, in fact a self-join, between account_id and account_parent, indicates that this is a Parent–Child dimension, as described in Chapter 13.)

This is the same column in the data source table:

account_id	account_description	account_rollup
1000	Assets	~
2000	Liabilities	~
3000	Net Sales	+
3100	Gross Sales	+
3200	Cost of Goods Sold	-
3300	Tax Refunds	+
3500	Return	-
4000	Total Expense	-
4100	General & Administration	+
4200	Information Systems	+
4300	Marketing	
4400	Lease	+
5000	Net Income	+
0		

Record: 14 ◀ | 14 | ▶ ▶▶ ▶* of 14

The unary operator for each member is in place. Figures for expenses and cost of goods sold, for example, are assigned minuses and those for net sales and net income are, among others, assigned pluses.

175

The sharp-eyed reader will have spotted that there's an entry under account_description for Marketing which has no operator in the account_rollup column. We'll see the effect this has in a moment....

With the operators in place, we need to tell the system to make use of them. With the Account Id level highlighted in the hierarchy, check out the last advanced property in the list. It's Unary Operators and is presently set to False (the default 'sum everything' behavior). Click the ellipsis button and the Define Unary Operator Column dialog opens:

Click to enable unary operators and, in this case, click to use an existing column, selecting account_rollup from the pop down list:

Click OK and the property is set to True. Save the change to the dimension and look at the data view of the members:

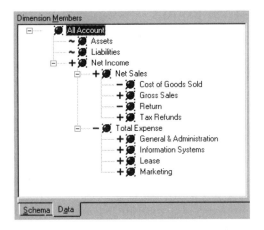

Each member now has an operator shown alongside it. Look at the last member, Marketing. Despite the lack of an operator in the account_rollup column, Marketing has gained a plus sign in the view above. If a blank value is found in the custom rollup column, the default behavior takes over again and the member is presumed to have a plus, or summing, unary operator.

Now look at the changes from the Cube Editor, first processing the cube. Suddenly things are looking pretty grim for the company:

Category	Current Year's Actuals	
Store	All Stores	
Time	1997	

		MeasuresLevel
- Level 02	+ Level 03	Amount
All Account	All Account Total	-$143,619.32
Assets		
Liabilities		
	Net Income Total	-$143,619.32
- Net Income	+ Net Sales	$22,863.12
	+ Total Expense	$166,482.44

Schema Data

With total expenses of $166,000-odd and net sales of just under $23,000, we're seeing a net income total of minus $143,000 – a horrible number but unfortunately correct.

Practical summary

Problem 2: Custom Rollup – when the cube's default behavior doesn't do the right job

Our expenses have been rolled up and added to sales, which is incorrect.

1 Create a new column (account_rollup) in the Account dimension table to hold the details of the custom rollup. *(This is done for you.)*
2 Add the appropriate unary operators as data in this column. *(This is done for you.)*
3 Edit the Account dimension. With the Account Id level highlighted in the hierarchy, and Advanced Properties selected, click the ellipsis button next to the Unary Operators property and, from the Define Unary Operator Column dialog, select the column account_rollup. Save and reprocess the dimension.
4 Reprocess the cube.

Problem 3: Custom Members – filling in missing information

Our third problem is that there is no budget information whatsoever in our cube. There is nothing in the fact table because it simply records facts such as sales, expenses and so on as generated by transactions in the operational database. Budget information is not generated by transactions in the same way. The upshot is that we have no budget data, and this is not helpful from a business perspective.

What can we do to address this? We can consider it under a general heading of 'calculations everywhere'. OLAP applications, and especially financial applications, will typically involve many, many calculations. They're used for forecasting, data modeling, allocations and so on – it's a very calculation-intensive environment. The solution to this widespread need for calculations is to allow the definition of a calculation for any member in the cube. In this case we want to define a calculation to produce our budget figures.

❡ *We've just mentioned 'calculations' and 'members' above so you might put them together and think about calculated members. There are, however, good reasons why we are not going to use calculated members. Firstly, a calculated member cannot have any levels or members below it and we may need subsidiary members for our*

budget data. Secondly, calculated members cannot have member properties and we saw in Chapter 11 how useful these can be for performing analyses. So, having considered all the angles, calculated members are not appropriate for this particular job. ❾

We need something different and it's an advanced property called Custom Members. Custom Members allow you to define the value of any member with an MDX expression and, once again, these expressions are stored in a separate column in the source database.

We'll use a very simple formula for our budget calculations because we are trying to show you how to set up a custom member rather than trying to do any real forecasting. So in our case the budget will be 110% of the previous year's actuals. Use the Dimension Editor to edit the `Category` dimension and with the Category Description highlighted in the Tree view, inspect the Advanced property called Custom Members. At present it's set to False, but clicking the ellipsis button opens the Define Custom Member Column. Checking the Enable Custom Members box lets you choose between a new or an existing column:

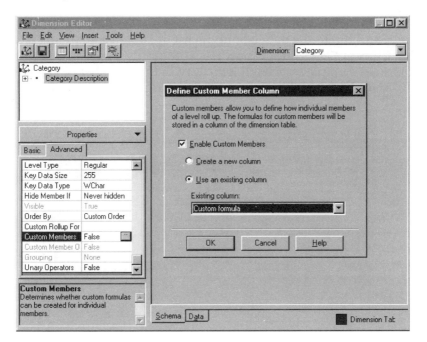

Being our usual helpful selves we've already defined a column in the data source called 'Custom formula':

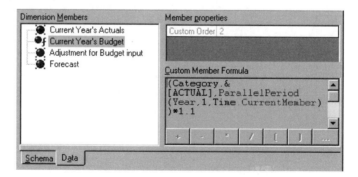

category_id	category_description	Custom formula
ACTUAL	Current Year's Actuals	
ADJUSTMENT	Adjustment for Budget input	
BUDGET	Current Year's Budget	(Category.&[ACTUAL],ParallelPeriod(Year,1,Time.CurrentMember))*1.1
FORECAST	Forecast	

The formula takes the actuals value from the previous year and multiplies it by 1.1, giving our budget of 110% of last year's actuals.

```
(Category.&[ACTUAL],ParallelPeriod(Year,1,
Time.CurrentMember))*1.1
```

❻ *The & in the formula indicates that the member **key** is being used to identify the member. In this case, as we have said, it is the* `category_id` *field that holds the member keys; see first row of the table above. There is more about this at the end of the chapter.* ❾

Click OK and flip to the data tab: in the list of Dimension Members you'll see that Current Year's Budget now has a little curly 'f' in front of it to show that there is a formula associated with it. With that member highlighted, in the Custom Member Formula pane (bottom right) you'll see the formula itself.

Save the changes to the dimension and process it. Now close the Dimension Editor and do a full reprocess on the cube. Finally browse the Budget cube with the Cube Editor. Our budget-calculating formula has worked and there's now a value – but that's the end of the good news:

Store	All Stores ▼
Time	1998 ▼
Account	All Account ▼

	MeasuresLevel
Category Description	Amount
Current Year's Actuals	-$868,910.74
Current Year's Budget	-$157,981.25
Adjustment for Budget inpi	
Forecast	

In 1998 the predicted losses were $158K and the actuals were nearer $870K.

❦ *Looks like the dot com collapse came early for our FoodMart company. The fact that it is an entirely fictitious company becomes more and more of a comfort.* ❦

And, just in case you were wondering, all of these changes should be visible in your chosen front-end tool.

Practical summary

Problem 3: Custom Members – filling in missing information

There is no budget information in our cube. There is nothing in the fact table because it simply records facts such as sales, expenses and so on as generated by transactions in the operational database. Budget information is not generated by transactions in the same way. We are going to create a Custom Member in the Category dimension. Custom Members allow you define the value of any members with an MDX expression and, once again, these expressions are stored in a separate column in the source database.

1 Create a new column (Custom Formula) in the Category dimension table to hold the details of the customized calculation. *(This is done for you.)*
2 Add the appropriate formula as data in this column. *(This is done for you.)*
3 Use the Dimension Editor to edit the Category dimension and with the Category Description highlighted in the Tree view, click the ellipsis button to the right of Custom Members. In the Define Custom Member Column dialog that opens, check the Enable Custom Members, Use an existing column and choose Custom Formula.
4 Save the changes and reprocess the dimension. Then reprocess the cube.

More about &

We said above that when you see an & (ampersand) in an MDX formula it indicates that the member key (rather than the member name) is being used to identify the member.

As we said earlier, the column in which member keys are found is one of the basic properties of a dimension, and for the Category dimension, the category_id column holds the member keys and the category_descrip-tion column holds the member names.

The ampersand (&) character is used in MDX to differentiate a member key from a member name, as you saw in the budget-generating expression used above:

```
(Category.&[ACTUAL],ParallelPeriod
(Year,1,Time.CurrentMember))*1.1
```

In this case, the member key [ACTUAL] is used.

category : Table

category_id	category_description
▶ ACTUAL	Current Year's Actuals
ADJUSTMENT	Adjustment for Budget input
BUDGET	Current Year's Budget
FORECAST	Forecast
*	

Referencing the member key ensures proper member identification in changing dimensions and in dimensions with non-unique member names.

❝ *A changing dimension is one with members that may move within the hierarchy. For instance, sales people move between stores or regions and a changing dimension lets you allocate the sales made by Employee X when working in Portland to the Portland store and, following a move to Spokane, to allocate sales to the Spokane store.* ❞

It turns out that the ampersand character can be used to indicate a member key reference in any MDX expression and often appears in machine-generated MDX. For example, if you build a query using ProClarity's GUI and then have a look at the MDX, you'll often find that it is using member key references rather than member name references, for example:

```
SELECT
{ [Time].&[1997] } ON COLUMNS ,
{ [Store].[Store State].&[CA], [Store].[Store State].&[OR],
[Store].[Store State].&[WA] } ON ROWS
FROM [Budget]
WHERE ( [Measures].[Amount] )
```

In practice you'll often find that the Member Key Column and the Member Name Column are pointing to the same column in the dimension table and hence to the same values.

In these cases you can safely remove the ampersands, secure in the knowledge that the MDX is still functional.

```
SELECT
{ [Time].[1997] } ON COLUMNS ,
{ [Store].[Store State].[CA], [Store].[Store State].[OR],
[Store].[Store State].[WA] } ON ROWS
FROM [Budget]
WHERE ( [Measures].[Amount] )
```

Summary

Well, the company may be going down fast but our MDX skills are on the up and up which should guarantee us employment, even if with another company.

1 We've looked at how you can control the order in which members appear on screen. This lets you present information to your users in a much more readable way.

2 Then we looked at how you can control the way in which child members are rolled up to form parent members. This ensures that you don't add, for example, Gross Sales and Returns to give Net Sales.

3 Finally we've looked at how you can create custom members which can be used, for example, for forecasting financial figures.

However, our budget cube still has some challenges remaining; these are dealt with in the next chapter.

Chapter 15

Further advanced data modeling techniques

Resources:

Starting database – either FoodMart2000_MDX3 if you completed the examples from the last chapter or FoodMart2000_EndChap14

Cube – Budget

Completed sample database – FoodMart2000_EndChap15

MDX samples – CHAP15.TXT

Write-enabled dimensions and working with data in other cubes

We're still using the Budget cube and in the last chapter we successfully dealt with three problems using Custom Order, Custom Rollup and Custom Members. However, this cube continues to have some problems and, by a remarkable stroke of good fortune, resolving those problems enables us to introduce you to some further MDX-related topics.

Fourthly (if you're counting from the top of the last chapter) when the cube was defined, an important, not to say essential, category of expense was omitted: salary.

Number five is that we have members called Cost of Goods Sold and Return in our Account dimension but there is no data for either in the cube.

Finally, number six, we're a little short of data – but more about this later.

We'll start with the missing salary member.

Problem 4: Write-enabled dimensions – allowing users to add a member to a dimension

Imagine that we have created the Budget cube and given the business users access to it. As always happens, as soon as they start to use it, they notice things that they forgot to tell us. The most important turns out to be one of the key expenses – salary.

This is quite a dilemma from the DBA's point of view. It would be possible to let that user edit the dimension table to add a new row for the salary data. This is not, however, a solution that is likely to win favor with a conscientious DBA who must retain an understanding of the cube structure in order to keep it running efficiently. An alternative is for the DBA to make the changes every time something gets forgotten, an equally unappealing option for the busy administrator. Is there any other solution?

Yes. (Inevitably.) The solution allows you (and specified users) to maintain the dimension and to modify its structure from within Analysis Manager. In many ways, it's a means of letting people work efficiently within their own fields of expertise. The DBA has one field of expertise and the business user has another so it makes sense to allow them to work together, the DBA taking care of major data issues and the business user adding business logic. Why particular figures are important and how they should be manipulated is not stuff a techie DBA is likely to find stimulating, and the finer points of scheduling incremental updates will probably bore a business user. So, how do we let specialists work in their own fields?

Dimensions have an advanced property called Write-enabled and in a write-enabled dimension, the administrators can change, move, add and delete members, and move members up and down levels in the hierarchy. Member property values can also be updated.

❝ *Once the Write-enabled property is set to True, not only does the administrator have these powers but so do any end-users allocated to cube roles with read/write access to the dimension. (This feature is available only with Analysis Services for Microsoft SQL Server 2000 Enterprise Edition.) For each role, you can control which members can and cannot be updated. Only Parent–Child dimensions can be write-enabled.* ❞

Adding a category of expense to the Account dimension in order to hold the salary figures means that our actions will ultimately modify the structure of the underlying table in the source database; so you may want to take a look at it before we proceed.

account_id	account_parent	account_description
1000		Assets
2000		Liabilities
3000	5000	Net Sales
3100	3000	Gross Sales
3200	3000	Cost of Goods Sold
3300	3000	Tax Refunds
3500	3000	Return
4000	5000	Total Expense
4100	4000	General & Administration
4200	4000	Information Systems
4300	4000	Marketing
4400	4000	Lease
5000		Net Income
0	0	

Account : Table

Record: 1 of 13

❝ *Not all of the columns are shown here, but there are enough to enable us to spot the changes that will be made.* ❞

Start by opening the Account dimension with the Dimension Editor and then look at the members of the dimension in the Data tab. Right click on a member and nothing happens: you cannot make any changes. This is the behavior we're about to alter. Now flip to the Schema tab and look at the advanced properties of the Account dimension. The Write-enabled property is set to False: click to select True.

Account
Account Id

Properties

Basic | Advanced

Default Member	
Depends On Dimension	(None)
Changing	True
Write-enabled	False
Member Keys Unique	True
Member Names Unique	False
Allow Duplicate Names	True

When you look at the Data tab, a message is shown saying 'Dimension write-back is unavailable until this dimension is included unmodified in a processed cube'. Dimension write-back is the process of writing any changes you make into the table in the source database.

In this case simply save and reprocess the dimension to clear this message in order to proceed. (This will work in most cases and, where it doesn't, reprocessing the Budget cube is all that is required in addition.) Now if you right click on a member, a menu pops out.

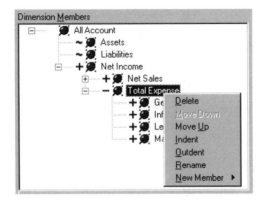

From this menu you can make changes to the hierarchy, moving members around the hierarchy using Move Up, Move Down, Indent and Outdent.

Moving these guys around isn't what we came here for, but just to give you a flavor of what is possible – indenting, for example, the Total Expense member makes it a child of Net Sales.

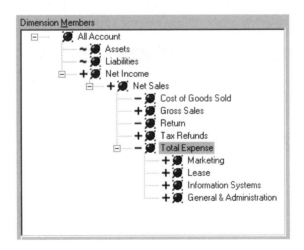

Outdenting it (from its original position) makes it a sibling of Net Income.

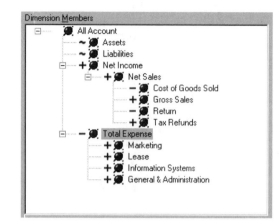

❡ *Sometimes when you indent and/or outdent, the order of the members appears to reverse (from alphabetical to reverse alphabetical). Fear not, this is only temporary; the order is restored when the dimension is saved.* ❡

Now we come to the option we want for our current task: New Member. Right click on Total Expenses and select New Member. A choice of Sibling or Child appears: we want Salary to be a child of Total Expenses. (If we'd started from, say, Marketing, the new member would be a Sibling.) Choose Child and a Create Member dialog opens; type in a name – Salary:

This dimension, being a Parent–Child dimension, is able to generate the member key automatically from the sequence in the account_id column in the Account table in the source database. Click OK

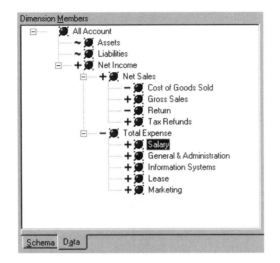

and there's the new member. It has gained the default summing behavior, indicated by the + unary operator, which is fine for our cube. Save the dimension, process it and close the Editor.

Once you've reached this stage, the changes you've made cannot be undone except by opening the Editor again and manually reversing them.

Inspect the Data view of the Budget cube with the Cube Editor and the new member is shown firmly in place, even though there isn't any data for it yet.

			MeasuresLevel
- Level 02	- Level 03	Level 04	Amount
All Account	All Account Total		-$143,619.32
Assets			
Liabilities			
	Net Income Total		-$143,619.32
	+ Net Sales	Net Sales Total	$22,863.12
		Total Expense Total	$166,482.44
- Net Income		General & Administration	$22,246.08
	- Total Expense	Information Systems	$44,713.80
		Lease	$32,661.60
		Marketing	$66,860.96
		Salary	

Schema Data

Just to check that the write back procedure is working, let's look at the Account table in the source database:

account_id	account_parent	account_description
1000		Assets
2000		Liabilities
3000	5000	Net Sales
3100	3000	Gross Sales
3200	3000	Cost of Goods Sold
3300	3000	Tax Refunds
3500	3000	Return
4000	5000	Total Expense
4100	4000	General & Administration
4200	4000	Information Systems
4300	4000	Marketing
4400	4000	Lease
5000		Net Income
5001	4000	Salary
0	0	

Account : Table

Record: 1 of 14

Yes, it's here too, which proves that our changes to the dimension have indeed been written back to the source database.

So, we have successfully set up a dimension such that users can edit dimensional structures.

❝ *Purely for information, everything we've done here using Analysis Manager's graphical user interface can also be achieved programmatically with an MDX statement that allows you to change dimensions. This is the ALTER CUBE CREATE DIMENSION MEMBER statement – so while it's easier to do it graphically as show, it is always comforting to know that you can also do it programmatically if necessary.* ❞

Practical summary

Problem 4: Write-enabled dimensions – allowing users to add a member to a dimension

1 Use the Dimension editor to examine the members of the Account dimension. Using the advanced properties of the Account dimension, set the Write-enabled property to True. Save and process the dimension.
2 Swap to the data tab. Right click on Total Expenses and select New Member. Choose Child and, in the Create Member dialog that opens, type in a name – Salary.
3 Save the dimension, process it and close the Editor.

Problem 5: Write-enabled dimensions – deriving values for a member using formulae

We have members called Cost of Goods Sold and Return in our Account dimension but there is no data in the cube. Equally there is no information in our fact table to tell us anything about the cost of goods sold or the percentage of our products that are returned. We need to derive the values for these members using formulae – both will be derived as a percentage of gross sales.

On the face of it, this sounds like much the same process that we demonstrated as the answer to the third problem in Chapter 14, when we put a formula in place to generate budget figures. However, this time we don't have a handy column in the dimension table that contains the formula. So, while it's true that we'll still be creating a custom member, we will be doing so in a different way.

We'll start by determining the formula to generate the cost of goods sold. We'll take advantage of the fact that we aren't dealing with a real company and make this really simple – the cost of goods sold is deemed to be 10% of gross sales and the return is 5% of gross sales. However, given the MDX skills you have already acquired, you could make it as complex as you need to meet the requirements of your business users.

In the Dimension Editor, looking at the Account dimension, highlight Account Id and then enable the Advanced Custom Members property as we did before. This time, as we don't have a column to hand, select the 'Create a new column' option and type in a name for it: we're using Custom Formula.

Click on OK.

> ❦ *That action will have created a new column in the Account table (in the source Access database) called* Custom Formula. ❦

Save and process the dimension (but don't leave the editor yet).

Now with the dimension write-enabled (which we did in the last section) and with custom members also now enabled, we can create a formula for any member in the dimension. In the Data tab, highlight the Cost of Goods Sold member and then click in the Custom Member Formula pane in the bottom right corner of the screen. Enter the formula

```
[Gross Sales]*0.1
```

and once you move the focus from the formula pane, the Cost of Goods Sold member acquires the curly f to show it's derived with a formula.

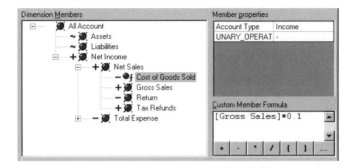

Now define a formula for the Return member: here's the formula:

    [Gross Sales]*0.05

and we're done. Save the dimension and call up the Cube Editor and browse the cube. But what's this? It looks exactly the same as before – there's still no data for Cost of Goods Sold or Return.

Category	Current Year's Actuals
Store	All Stores
Time	1997

- Level 02	- Level 03	Level 04	MeasuresLevel
			Amount
All Account	All Account Total		-$143,619.32
Assets			
Liabilities			
	Net Income Total		-$143,619.32
		Net Sales Total	$22,863.12
		Cost of Goods Sold	
- Net Income	- Net Sales	Gross Sales	
		Return	
		Tax Refunds	$22,863.12
	+ Total Expense	Total Expense Total	$166,482.44

Schema Data

And come to think of it, we still don't have any data for salaries either.... What's gone wrong?

Let's address those questions in reverse order. Why is there no salary data? It's because this is a budget cube and the fact table from which it takes its information simply doesn't contain any salary data.

And why are there no figures for returns or cost of good sold? These figures are both derived as percentages of the gross sales figure – which gives us not an answer but another question: why are there no gross sales figures?

Once again, the answer is because we are dealing with a budget cube and it does not contain any values for gross sales. So let's summarize what we **did** achieve in this step and then we'll address these final problems.

Practical summary

Problem 5: Write-enabled dimensions – deriving values for a member using formulae

1 With the Dimension Editor, look at the Account dimension, highlight Account Id and enable the Advanced Custom Members property. Select 'Create a new column' and name it 'Custom Formula'.
2 Save and process the dimension.
3 In the Data tab, highlight the Cost of Goods Sold member and click in the Custom Member Formula pane. Enter the formula to calculate Cost of Goods Sold.
4 Repeat step 3 for the Return member.

Problem 6: Missing data – bringing it in from other cubes

Most business applications will involve more than one cube. We've been working with the Budget cube but there are also likely to be other cubes to hand. In our example, the FoodMart2000_MDX3 database contains several cubes: there are also cubes called HR (Human Resources) and Sales. The HR cube contains the details of members of staff: their names, positions, the date they were hired, the store and department in which they work and, of course, their salaries. The Sales cube contains information about the products, their manufacturers, prices, the department within a store where they're on sale, information about each store and details of all transactions – who bought what when and for how much.

These HR and Sales cubes contain the vital information we need to complete our Budget cube: HR has salary values and Sales has gross sales values. So we need to get that data from one cube into another.

To complete our Budget cube we need to bring figures in from other cubes in the database. The term that describes this process is 'connected multi-cube architecture'.

❛ *It is terms like these that can help to justify that salary increase you know you are worth.*

"Well, I don't know. (Slow head shake). To solve that one we're going to have to develop a connected multi-cube architecture. As you know, that usually means an expensive consultant. However, given the right incentive I just might be able to..."

In practice all it means is that we're able to define a calculation in one cube that references data in another cube. (For a small fee, we won't tell your boss how simple it is). ❜

To do this we use an MDX function called LookUpCube which works with any cube within a database. LookUpCube has two parameters; the first is the name of the cube from which you wish to import data. The second parameter is a string that has to evaluate into an MDX expression that refers to a certain cell in the cube providing the values.

Return to editing the Account dimension where we'll create formulas for the gross sales and salary members. This will be much the same as we've just done for cost of goods sold and return, but this time we'll be using the new function. Click on the Gross Sales member in the Data view and in the Custom Member Formula pane we'll construct the formula. As before, we'll build it up a bit at a time. So we'll start with:

```
LookUpCube (("[Sales]","(Measures.[Sales],
```

We've given LookUpCube the name of the cube from which it's to fetch data – Sales – and have started to specify where in the cube it will find the values we want. The function requires this information in the form of a string, hence the inverted commas. So far we've told it to look at the Sales measure.

Next, we must direct it to exactly the same place in the Sales cube as we are in the Budget cube. The values for gross sales are at intersections of the Time dimension and the Store dimension so we take the current time and append it to the string, like this:

```
LookUpCube("[Sales]","(Measures.[Sales],
Time.["+Time.CurrentMember.Name+"],
```

We are, in fact, concatenating the string; that is, combining multiple strings into a single one using the plus symbol. Now we do the same for the Store dimension and here's the complete formula:

```
LookUpCube("[Sales]","(Measures.[Sales],
Time.["+Time.CurrentMember.Name+"],
Store.["+Store.CurrentMember.Name+"])")
```

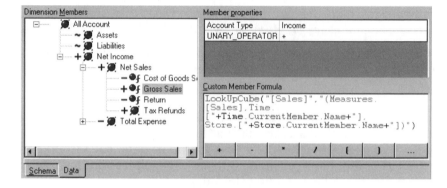

Save the dimension and process it. Then process the Budget cube and look at it with the Cube Editor and, wonderfully, there is now a figure for gross sales. Equally wonderfully, the formulae for Cost of Goods Sold and Return now have a Gross Sales value with which to work and also display values.

			MeasuresLevel
· Level 02	· Level 03	Level 04	Amount
All Account	All Account Total		$336,833.09
Assets			
Liabilities			
	Net Income Total		$336,833.09
		Net Sales Total	$503,315.53
		Cost of Goods Sold	$56,523.81
· Net Income	· Net Sales	Gross Sales	$565,238.13
		Return	$28,261.91
		Tax Refunds	$22,863.12
	+ Total Expense	Total Expense Total	$166,482.44

These are the figures for 1997.

It's easy to see that the formula for Cost of Goods Sold is working as it's 10% of the gross sales figure. We can also see that the figure for Return is half of that for cost of goods sold, and again we know that's right because the formula for Return was 5% of Gross Sales.

Spurred on by this success, we'll create another custom member formula to bring the salaries values in from the HR cube in just the same way, using this formula:

```
LookUpCube("[HR]","(Measures.[Org Salary],
Time.["+Time.CurrentMember.Name+"],
Store.["+Store.CurrentMember.Name+"])")
```

Back in the Cube Editor, we can see that now, at last, we have all the values needed by the cube and its users.

- Level 02	- Level 03	Level 04	MeasuresLevel Amount
	Net Income Total		$297,401.42
		Net Sales Total	$503,315.53
		Cost of Goods Sold	$56,523.81
	- Net Sales	Gross Sales	$565,238.13
		Return	$28,261.91
- Net Income		Tax Refunds	$22,863.12
		Total Expense Total	$205,914.11
		General & Administration	$22,246.08
	- Total Expense	Information Systems	$44,713.80
		Lease	$32,661.60
		Marketing	$66,860.96
		Salary	$39,431.67

Schema   Data

Practical summary

Problem 6: Missing data – bringing it in from other cubes

1 Edit the Account dimension with the Dimension editor. Click on the Gross Sales member in the Data view and in the Custom Member Formula pane, construct the formula to bring in data from the Sales cube.

2 Save the dimension and process it. Process the Budget cube and inspect it with the Cube Editor.

3 Repeat steps 1 and 2 for the Salary member, bringing in data from the HR (Human Resources) cube.

Summary

We've brought our cube on a long way in the course of this chapter and the net effect is a much more flexible cube which should require less maintenance to keep it in shape.

1 We've given certain users permission to edit a dimension, making use of the Write-enable property to do so. This gives users control over aspects of the data where their expertise is strongest.

2 Then we created some custom members to calculate data that was needed in the cube. Deriving data from data that's already in the cube adds flexibility, giving users the figures they need at their fingertips.

3 Finally we used LookUpCube to pull data from other cubes in the database into our budget cube. LookUpCube is an advanced and very powerful function that helps keep your cubes controllable. The LookUpCube function is an efficient way to bring data from one cube into another, in terms of both time and effort. It's easier to manage a range of cubes covering different aspects of your business data and it also means that data does not have to be stored multiple times.

Function	Requires	Returns
LookUpCube	Cube name, string expression	Values from another cube

Chapter 16

Actions

Resources:

Starting database – `FoodMart2000_MDX3`
Cube – `Sales`
MDX samples – `CHAP16.TXT`

An action, according to the MDX function list in Analysis Services' help system, is an operation that can be initiated by an end user upon a selected cube or portion of a cube. Right, fine – but what does it mean? This is one occasion where a 'for instance' is worth its weight in help system entries, so here we go.

Imagine (for instance) that you are a high level analyst browsing through the data about all of FoodMart's stores and your present concern is stock levels in the American stores. You drill down to USA and down again into Washington state. Browsing around, you see a city with a curious name – Walla Walla. You didn't know of the existence of this place and it's news to you that FoodMart has a store there, store number 22, in fact. Your curiosity piqued, you want to know more about this euphonious location. You right click on Store 22 and from the pop out menu, you select Show Map.

This should work from any front-end tool that is well enough integrated with Analysis Services. It works fine from within ProClarity:

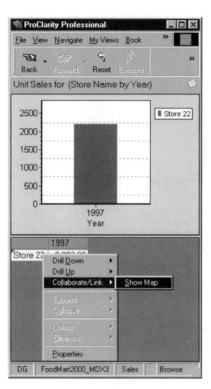

In addition, it works from within the Cube Editor:

WA Total		124,366.00
+ Bellingham	Bellingham Total	2,237.00
+ Bremerton	Bremerton Total	24,576.00
+ Seattle	Seattle Total	25,011.00
+ Spokane	Spokane Total	23,591.00
+ Tacoma	Tacoma Total	35,257.00
- Walla Walla	Walla Walla Total	2,203.00
	Store 22	2,203.00
+ Yakima	Yakima To	.00

Drill Down
Drill Up
Member Properties...
Show Map

Your browser is launched and brings back a map from Yahoo which shows the location of Walla Walla with a red star, tucked into the south eastern corner of the state and close to the Oregon border.

❦ *This worked fine when we tested it but, as you can imagine, we can't guarantee that Yahoo will continue, in perpetuity, to offer this fine service. If this doesn't work for you, try altering the URL string that we show you later on in the chapter to point to a web address that you know to be operational. It doesn't have to do mapping in order to demonstrate the general principle that actions can launch browsers.* ❧

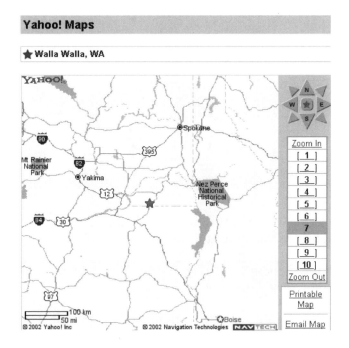

A bit of zooming reveals:

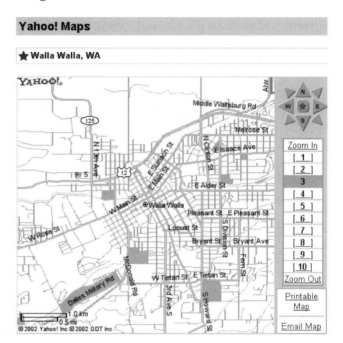

So now you know the whereabouts of Walla Walla, even if you are not yet aware that it means 'many waters' in the Nez Percé tongue.

❛ *Given that, as the screen shots show, it is located in WA, one is left wondering how "Walla Walla Wa" would translate...* ❜

So, that was an Action in... er... action. Actions permit users to remain within the analysis environment while locating pertinent information, as in the scenario above, or furthering the process of analysis by involving others. As another example, imagine you've found some interesting piece of information, perhaps that sales in a particular store have slumped dramatically. What happens now? You'll probably do one of several things, like picking up the phone and calling somebody, or walking down the hall and talking to someone about it, or sending an email. All these things take you out of the analysis environment and require you to open up a separate application or to go and perform some other deed. Actions let you maintain the flow of analysis: when you reach a point where you find something interesting you can act upon it instantly with minimal distraction.

An action can, as we've said, go and locate information from the web or from an intranet, and the different kinds of action can launch different applications and retrieve different types of information. An action can also bring flexibility to working with cubes. You could, for instance, create an action that would place an order for an item with your supplier. This action could be selected if a low stock level was found while browsing stock levels.

MDX is used to define actions and there are several types of action from which to choose. The map-finding example above is a URL action; there are six others including HTML actions that execute an HTML script within a web browser and Data Set actions that will return a multi dimensional set of data. We'll take you through one worked example of an action (using URLs). The other actions are used in much the same way, so we'll simply show you how to find them (using a wizard) and leave you to investigate once you're familiar with the general idea.

So let's go behind the scenes to see how the map-finding action was defined. Look at the Sales cube with the Cube Editor and in the tree pane you can see an action listed.

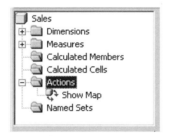

Right click on Show Map and select Edit. We'll walk you through how it was put together.

❧ *After that, if you want to, you can delete Show Map and re-create it for yourself, using exactly the same steps.* ❧

First you choose the object from which you wish to launch the action: this object is called, somewhat counter-intuitively, the target. There are several different objects that can be used as targets ranging from the whole cube through a dimension, level, member, cell or set. In our map-finding example, we want a right click on any store number at the Store Name level to act as the target. The object that will act as the target is, therefore, any member at a level in the cube, so the target is set to 'A level in this cube'. Next, we specify the dimension to which the target level belongs – Store – and the level itself – Store Name. Lastly we specify that it is to be the members at the chosen level that will act as the target. Then click on Next.

Action Wizard

Select target

Choose the cube object that you want to define as the target of this action.

Target: A level in this cube

Select a dimension to which the level belongs.

Dimension: Store

Select a level in this dimension.

Levels: Store Name

Define the target as:

(•) Members of the selected level

( ) The level object

< Back   Next >   Cancel   Help

In the second step of the wizard, we choose the action type.

Action Wizard

Select the action type

Choose the type for this action. These predefined action types allow client applications to perform actions without needing to understand the nature or syntax of the action.

Type: URL

Description
A URL that can be launched using an Internet browser.

Sample:
Defines an action that uses an Internet browser to search for the current member in the Store dimension using the MSN search engine:

"http://search.msn.com/results.asp?q=" + [Store].CurrentMember.Name

| < Back | Next > | Cancel | Help |

As discussed, it is a URL action. The Sample pane at the bottom of the screen helpfully shows the sort of syntax that's required by the chosen action type: in this case it is a URL string which will be sent to the web browser.

❡ *The other actions at your disposal are revealed by popping down the combo box.*

URL

Command Line
Statement
HTML
URL
Data set
Rowset
Proprietary

❡

Click on Next and in the next step, the Syntax pane shows the MDX code that is at the heart of our URL action:

The MDX reads as:

```
Iif(Ancestor([Store].CurrentMember,[Store].[Store
Country]).Name="USA","http://maps.yahoo.com/py/
Maps.py?Pyt=Tmap&addr=&csz="+[Store].CurrentMember.Parent.Name
+","+Ancestor([Store].CurrentMember,[Store].[Store
State]).Name,"")
```

It looks complicated but, like most MDX, as soon as you dismantle it, everything is revealed.

For a start, we're using " to indicate literal strings and + as a concatenation operator (which essentially glues strings together).

Also note we are using four MDX functions. Three of these we've seen before: Iif (Chapter 8), Parent and Ancestor (Chapter 6).

❧ *Just to remind you, the Iif function takes three parameters: a condition to be evaluated, what's to be done if the condition is met and what's to be done if it's not met. Parent, when given a member, will return that member's parent, while Ancestor requires the member in which you're interested and the level at which you want to find its ancestor.* ❧

208

The new function is Name which will return the name of a level, dimension, member, or hierarchy. The general syntax is:

```
<<Dimension>>.Name
<<Level>>.Name
<<Member>>.Name
<<Hierarchy>>.Name
```

for example:

```
Store.[Store Country].Name
```

OK, given that background information, let's pull the statement apart. We'll work from the inside out – so we'll ignore the Iif and remove it for now. This leaves us with an intermediate expression:

```
"Http://maps.yahoo.com/py/maps.py?Pyt=Tmap&addr=&csz="
+[Store].CurrentMember.Parent.Name+","
+Ancestor([Store].CurrentMember,[Store].[Store State]).Name
```

When the action is initiated, we want to direct the browser to Yahoo's maps. This is the HTTP string to do just that:

```
http://maps.yahoo.com/py/maps.py?Pyt=Tmap&addr=&csz=
```

so this will eventually be sent to the browser. However, we happen to know that Yahoo's mapping program also requires the name of a city and a state to be entered so that it can show the correct map. No problem, we can get this information from the cube. It also happens to need those two separated by a comma.

First we need to get the name of the city. Oh, that's lucky, we just introduced the Name function, so we can use that:

```
Store.CurrentMember.Parent.Name
```

Here the Name function returns the name of the parent of the current member in the Store dimension. (Checking the hierarchy, shown below, we see that our current member is at the Store Name level and above it sits the name of the city at the Store City level).

· Store Country	· Store State	· Store City	Store Name
		+ Spokane	Spokane Total
		+ Tacoma	Tacoma Total
· USA	· WA	· Walla Walla	Walla Walla Total
			Store 22
		+ Yakima	Yakima Total

The Parent function returns Walla Walla, being the parent of Store 22, and its actual name is returned by the Name function.

So, we've got our literal HTTP string and we've got the name of the store, and we concatenated the two using +.

Now for the state:

```
Ancestor([Store].CurrentMember,[Store].[Store State]).Name
```

This time the Name function returns the name of the ancestor of the current member at the Store State level. The ancestor of Store 22 at the Store State level is Washington. Finally, slot in the comma that's required between the city and the state.

So, to recap, our intermediate expression:

```
"Http://maps.yahoo.com/py/maps.py?Pyt=Tmap&addr=&csz="
+[Store].CurrentMember.Parent.Name+","
+Ancestor([Store].CurrentMember,[Store].[Store State]).Name
```

evaluates to a string like this:

```
Http://maps.yahoo.com/py/maps.py?Pyt=Tmap&addr=&csz=
Walla Walla,Washington
```

which is sent to the browser.

❛ *This works fine although, in fact, the browser, which is not too keen on spaces in HTTP, will translate this to:*

```
Http://maps.yahoo.com/py/maps.py?Pyt=Tmap&addr=&csz=
Walla%20Walla,Washington
```
❜

This is enough to get us to a map of Walla Walla.

Our intermediate expression works fine just as it is; you can try it if you like. So, why have we complicated it with an Iif statement?

If we compress the entire statement and turn part of it into pseudo code, this hopefully becomes clear:

```
Iif(Ancestor([Store].CurrentMember,[Store].[Store
Country]).Name="USA", then do the intermediate statement,
otherwise do nothing)
```

The Ancestor expression finds the ancestor of the current member in the Store dimension at the StoreCountry level, uses the Name function to return its name and then checks to see if that name is equal to USA. In our scenario we only have access to maps of the United States via Yahoo, so the action is designed to work only for stores in the USA. If the store is not in the United States, then we do not want anything to happen, which is the purpose of the "" at the end of the statement.

Here's the expression again in its entirety:

```
Iif(Ancestor([Store].CurrentMember,[Store].[Store
Country]).Name="USA","http://maps.yahoo.com/py/maps.py?Pyt
=Tmap&addr=&csz="+[Store].CurrentMember.Parent.Name+","
+Ancestor([Store].CurrentMember,[Store].[Store
State]).Name,"")
```

OK, that hopefully explains the MDX expression, now back to the wizard. The last step of the wizard shows a summary description of the action.

If you were building the action from scratch, you'd click Finish after checking the summary but as we're just looking – and you may well have played with the wizard's options while we've been working our way through (an excellent way to learn) – click Cancel to leave the action in its original state.

That's just one illustration of the power of actions and although relatively simple, it's a graphic demonstration of how users can be given fascinating resources at their mousetips.

Chapter 17

Server side color coding

Resources:

Starting database – `Coloring Sample`
Cube – `Budget`
Completed sample database – `FoodMart2000_EndChap17`
MDX samples – `CHAP17.TXT`

Color coding is a means of guiding the users' investigation of a cube by using colors to bring attention to certain values. You may have come across something similar in Excel: in a stock control spreadsheet for instance, as soon as a value for stock holding drops below a certain level, that value can be displayed in red, making it much easier to spot and reducing the likelihood of running out of stock completely. Color coding in Analysis Services is broadly similar – making it easier to spot patterns, trends or a value that has drifted from the norm.

However, bear in mind that multi-dimensional cubes are typically more complex than spreadsheets. Each measure can be viewed from the perspective of many different dimensions. In addition, those dimensions will commonly have many levels so the potentially problematical values may be several levels deep in the hierarchy.

Incidentally, color coding has been implemented on the server itself. There are two reasons for this: the first is that by managing the color coding on the server, it is available for many front-end client applications. So long as the client supports color coding (not all do as yet), you'll be able to make use of this feature.

Secondly, we want the color coding to work at all levels within a dimension's hierarchy. To transfer this to the client would mean sending over large amounts of data for evaluation each time a drilling down or up operation took place. The decision to keep color coding on the server keeps the transfer of data to a minimum, improving response times and reducing network traffic.

Now let's do some practical work. Imagine you had a calculated measure that worked out the variance between the budget figures and the actual figures, in order to gauge performance against the budget. You could apply a color coding scheme to this value so that high deviations from budget are distinguished by a red background, medium deviations by yellow and low by green.

Let's do this. The Budget cube has a dimension called Category and we want to see our variance figures as part of this dimension. First, for practice, create a calculated measure which works out the variance. In the Cube Editor, right click on the Calculated Members folder and select New Calculated Member. Set its parent dimension to be Category, the Parent member to be All Category and give it the name V%.

For the MDX expression, we want to take the current year's actuals, subtract them from the current year's budget and divide that figure by the current year's actuals. This gives us the percentage difference between actuals and budget. We'll use the Iif function, as introduced in Chapter 8, to do this.

The first thing Iif needs is a condition to evaluate. We want to evaluate two conditions, which we can do by putting an 'and' between them. We want to find out if the cells containing actuals have content and whether that content is less than or greater than zero. This is the code thus far:

```
Iif ( [Current Year's Actuals] <> 0 and NOT
IsEmpty([Current Year's Actuals]),
```

You could also put these conditions in reverse order, like this:

```
Iif (NOT IsEmpty([Current Year's Actuals] and
[Current Year's Actuals] <> 0),
```

Next, Iif needs to know what to do if the condition is met (found to be true). We want it to take the actuals figure, subtract the budget figure from it and divide the result by the actuals figure. This works out the variance of the actuals figures from the budget figures. Iif's third requirement is what to do if the condition evaluates to false: we want it to do nothing. This is the complete statement:

```
Iif ( [Current Year's Actuals] <> 0 and NOT
IsEmpty([Current Year's Actuals]),
([Current Year's Actuals] - [Current Year's Budget]) /
[Current Year's Actuals], Null)
```

and here it is in the Calculated Member Builder:

Calculated Member Builder		
Parent dimension:	Category	▼
Parent member:	[All Category]	Change...
Member name:	V%	
		Check
Value expression		

```
Iif ( [Current Year's Actuals] <> 0 and NOT IsEmpty
([Current Year's Actuals]),
([Current Year's Actuals] - [Current Year's Budget]) /
[Current Year's Actuals], Null)
```

Check the syntax and save the calculated member.

Have a look at the advanced properties for your new calculated member and, because we want the value to display as a percentage, set the format string to Percent.

It is worth, at this point, taking a bit of time to browse through the data to get a feel for what this calculated member is doing.

	MeasuresLevel	Category Description	
		Amount	
+ Store Country	Current Year's Actuals	Current Year's Budget	V%
All Stores	$398,755.69	$565,238.13	-41.75%
+ Canada	$0.00		
+ Mexico	$0.00		
+ USA	$398,755.69	$565,238.13	-41.75%

Schema Data

Using an arithmetical assistant of choice, you can subtract the USA budget from the actuals, divide the result by the actuals and get the answer of –41.75%. If you expand USA so that you can see the states and try the same calculation for, say, Oregon, your assistant should agree with the V% figure of –21.91%.

		MeasuresLevel	Category Description	
			Amount	
- Store Country	+ Store State	Current Year's Actuals	Current Year's Budget	V%
All Stores	All Stores Total	$398,755.69	$565,238.13	-41.75%
+ Canada	Canada Total	$0.00		
+ Mexico	Mexico Total	$0.00		
	USA Total	$398,755.69	$565,238.13	-41.75%
- USA	+ CA	$71,980.16	$159,167.84	-121.13%
	+ OR	$116,702.19	$142,277.07	-21.91%
	+ WA	$210,073.34	$263,793.22	-25.57%

Schema Data

The new calculated member is happily working at all levels.

The next step is to add the color coding: inspecting the advanced properties of your new calculated member reveals a BackColor property.

This is where we get our hands on the paintbox albeit in a rather esoteric fashion.

Firstly, we'll introduce a couple of functions that may be familiar to VBA programmers. One is Abs which returns absolute numbers (numbers shorn of signs indicating plus or minus values). Its syntax is:

```
Abs(number)
```

The second function is RGB. It stands for Red Green Blue and is a means of controlling colors by specifying their red, green and blue components and is used like this:

```
RGB(255,0,0)
```

for example, is the code for the color red.

Now we'll discuss the game plan. The result we want is for the background of the cells containing the variance percentage to change color depending on the value.

= 0	White
> 0 and < 25	Green
=> 25 and < 50	Yellow
=> 50	Red

We start by finding the maximum value in the set of descendants of the current member in the Store dimension, and we want this to be done regardless of the current member we're focusing upon. In other words, find the descendants of whichever member currently has the focus.

❥ *You may be wondering why we are bothering to find the maximum value of the **descendants** of the current member. All will be revealed in the fullness of time...*

Then we take the absolute number of the current member in the Category dimension.

❥ *We are taking the absolute value because that is always positive and you'll notice, in the expression below, that we perform the comparison with a positive number.* ❦

If this number is greater than or equal to 0.5, we want to use red as the background color. All this is to be wrapped up inside an Iif function, so the start of our expression looks like this:

```
Iif( Max ({Descendants([Store].CurrentMember),
[Store].CurrentMember},
Abs([Category].CurrentMember)) >= .5, RGB(255,0,0), //red
```

In English this reads as "If the value of any of the descendants of the current member exceeds 0.5 then turn the background of the current member red."

Two slashes – // – denote a comment. Here we're putting in comments to translate the colors from numbers to more readily understood words as an aid to easier understanding of the expression. As you start to use MDX for more and more complex tasks, comments become more and more useful both to you and to anyone else who has to maintain your code.

We'll need to nest another two Iif functions inside our expression to accommodate all four of the color options so the expression continues as follows:

```
Iif( Max ({Descendants([Store].CurrentMember),
[Store].CurrentMember},
Abs([Category].CurrentMember)) >= .25,RGB(255,255,0), // yellow
Iif( Max ({Descendants([Store].CurrentMember),
[Store].CurrentMember},
Abs([Category].CurrentMember)) > 0, RGB(0,255,0), //green
RGB(255,255,255)))) //white
```

The expression looks complex in its entirety but once you've conquered the first Iif, it's mainly a case of repeating the pattern with different values and not forgetting the final "what to do if the conditions evaluated by all three Iifs are found to be false" (that's the RGB(255,255,255) at the end) followed by the closing braces for all three Iif functions.

To continue with the practicalities, return to a state where you're inspecting the advanced properties of the V% calculated member from the Cube Editor. With the BackColor property highlighted, click the ellipsis button to open the MDX Builder. This is where you construct the expression described above. For completeness' sake, here's the whole expression:

```
Iif( Max ({Descendants([Store].CurrentMember),
[Store].CurrentMember},
Abs([Category].CurrentMember)) >= .5, RGB(255,0,0), //red
Iif( Max ({Descendants([Store].CurrentMember),
[Store].CurrentMember},
Abs([Category].CurrentMember)) >= .25,RGB(255,255,0), // yellow
Iif( Max ({Descendants([Store].CurrentMember),
[Store].CurrentMember},
Abs([Category].CurrentMember)) > 0, RGB(0,255,0), //green
RGB(255,255,255)))) //white
```

Click OK when you've finished and the expression is pasted automatically as the `BackColor` property. Save the cube and inspect the Data tab. This is the result: in glorious monochrome it doesn't pack quite the punch we hoped for but it glows beautifully on a monitor.

+ Store Country	Category Description V%
All Stores	-41.75%
+ Canada	
+ Mexico	
+ USA	-41.75%

Schema Data

You can drill down into the store hierarchy and the color coding continues to work:

- Store Country	- Store State	+ Store City	Category Description V%
All Stores	All Stores Total		-41.75%
+ Canada	Canada Total		
+ Mexico	Mexico Total		
- USA	USA Total		-41.75%
	+ CA	CA Total	-121.13%
	- OR	OR Total	-21.91%
		+ Portland	-24.19%
		+ Salem	-20.52%
	+ WA	WA Total	-25.57%

Schema Data

Or does it? The USA total is –41.75% and is shown in red, but didn't we decide to use red as the background color when the variance is over 50%?

Yes, but we also want the color coding to be 'intelligent'. It may be that there are poor figures (i.e. figures of 50% or greater) buried deep down inside a hierarchy. We want to be able to find them easily so we have constructed the MDX expression so that the color of its background is dependant on the largest figure that is found in all of its descendants. This explains the part of the expression that reads:

```
Iif( Max ({Descendants([Store].CurrentMember),
[Store].CurrentMember},
Abs([Category].CurrentMember)) >= .5, RGB(255,0,0), //red
```

"If the value of any of the descendants of the current member equals or exceeds 0.5 then turn the current member red."

So, when we see that the USA total is –41.75% (which is bad enough) the red color tells us that there is worse lurking below. Somewhere in the lower levels one value (or more) falls into the 50% or over band. If we drill down, we can see that the problem lies with Alameda, and going further down to the Store Name level shows us that this isn't a store that's performing badly, it's our very own Headquarters.

- Store Country	- Store State	- Store City	Store Name	Category Description
				V%
+ Mexico	Mexico Total			
	USA Total			-41.75%
		CA Total		-121.13%
		- Alameda	Alameda Total	100.00%
			HQ	100.00%
- USA	- CA	+ Beverly Hills	Beverly Hills Total	-26.44%
		+ Los Angeles	Los Angeles Total	-22.40%
		+ San Diego	San Diego Total	-23.26%
		+ San Francisco	San Francisco Total	-23.57%
	+ OR	OR Total		-21.91%
	+ WA	WA Total		-25.57%

Schema Data

How ironic. All our stores are managing to at least keep the budget in sight while headquarters appears to be ignoring it completely.

Summary

We hope we've demonstrated the value of color coding in this very simple example that allows us to identify an area with a problem quickly. You can imagine in a more complex example in a cube with maybe ten dimensions and many more levels, finding this problem could be much more challenging without the aid of color coding.

Chapter 18

More about querying

Resources:

Starting database – `FoodMart_MDX1`
Cube – `Sales_MDX1`
MDX samples – `CHAP18.TXT`

In Chapter 3 we used queries to introduce the general syntax used in MDX. As we said in that chapter, most of the time people use some form of GUI tool to query the cube, so they won't be writing MDX queries by hand. Nevertheless, we have included this chapter on more advanced querying for three reasons.

1 Even if you use a front-end tool, you may want to look at the MDX it generates, so a greater understanding of queries should help you to understand what the code is doing.
2 There is still a bit of core information that we feel the need to impart about how MDX works and queries are the easiest way to demonstrate it.
3 We happen to find this stuff generally interesting and we thought you might too.

Named sets

You can, if such takes your fancy, give names to specific sets and then use those names in the query.

For example:

```
With Set [Kids] AS
'{[Product].[All Products].Children}'
SELECT {[Kids]} ON COLUMNS ,
{ [Unit Sales] } ON ROWS
FROM [Sales_MDX1]
```

is functionally the equivalent of:

```
SELECT {[Product].[All Products].Children} ON COLUMNS ,
{ [Unit Sales] } ON ROWS
FROM [Sales_MDX1]
```

In this case we'd have to admit that the use of a named set is no major advantage; however, their use can be a boon to readability in large complex queries.

CROSSJOIN

By the end of Chapter 3 we had shown you how to write a query that could display data from two of the dimensions using COLUMNS and ROWS. But what happens if you (or your users) want to use two dimensions on the same axis? To demonstrate what we mean by 'two dimensions on the same axis' we'll start off with a simple query that only uses one dimension on each axis:

```
SELECT
{ [Time].[1997].CHILDREN } ON COLUMNS ,
{[Product].[All Products].Children} ON ROWS
FROM [Sales_MDX1]
WHERE ( [Measures].[Unit Sales] )
```

which produces a grid like this:

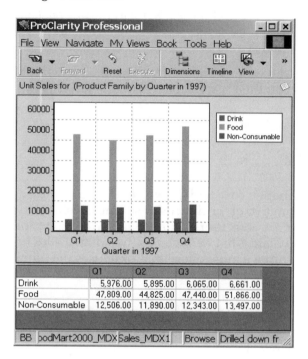

❝ *We've included bar charts as well in the screen shots, but the MDX is probably easier to understand if you concentrate on the grid initially.* ❞

But suppose we want to see the products analyzed by time **and** by state? Something like this:

```
ProClarity Professional                          _ □ ×
File  View  Navigate  My Views  Book  Tools  Help

Back  Forward  Reset  Execute  Dimensions  Timeline  View      »
```

Unit Sales for (Quarter in 1997)

[Chart showing Quarter in 1997 with legend: CA/Drink, CA/Food, CA/Non-Consumable, OR/Drink, OR/Food, OR/Non-Consumable, WA/Drink, WA/Food, WA/Non-Consumable; y-axis 0 to 30000, x-axis Q1 Q2 Q3 Q4]

		Q1	Q2	Q3	Q4
CA	Drink	1,654.00	1,608.00	1,792.00	2,048.00
	Food	12,064.00	13,074.00	13,135.00	15,383.00
	Non-Consumable	3,172.00	3,370.00	3,443.00	4,005.00
OR	Drink	1,643.00	1,478.00	1,486.00	1,499.00
	Food	13,737.00	10,726.00	12,325.00	11,749.00
	Non-Consumable	3,907.00	2,875.00	3,129.00	3,105.00
WA	Drink	2,679.00	2,809.00	2,787.00	3,114.00
	Food	22,008.00	21,025.00	21,980.00	24,734.00
	Non-Consumable	5,427.00	5,645.00	5,771.00	6,387.00

```
BB  oodMart2000_MDX Sales_MDX1    Browse  Drilled down fror
```

What we need to do here is to modify the part of the query that specifies the rows. For each of the four quarters in 1997 we want a row that shows each product type for each state. So, for example, if we had two product types and two states, we'd want to see four rows; with five product types and five states, we want to see 25 and so on.

OK, how do we do it? In fact there are two syntactical alternatives we can use in MDX to achieve this. They are:

```
SELECT
{ [Time].[1997].Children } ON COLUMNS ,
CROSSJOIN ({ [Store].[Store Country].[USA].Children } ,
{[Product].[All Products].Children}) ON ROWS
FROM [Sales_MDX1]
WHERE ( [Measures].[Unit Sales] )
```

and/or

```
SELECT
{ [Time].[1997].Children } ON COLUMNS ,
{{ [Store].[Store Country].[USA].Children } * {[Product].[All
Products].Children}} ON ROWS
FROM [Sales_MDX1]
WHERE ( [Measures].[Unit Sales] )
```

In our example the set

```
{ [Store].[Store Country].[USA].Children }
```

returns three members from the Store dimension – CA, OR and WA – and the set:

```
{[Product].[All Products].Children}
```

also returns three members – Drink, Food and Non-Consumables.
The results from each set are multiplied together to give the nine rows that we see.

Of course you can play around with these statements to your heart's content. You can, for example, try a crossjoin on the columns:

```
SELECT
CROSSJOIN ({ [Store].[Store Country].[USA].Children } ,
{[Product].[All Products].Children}) ON COLUMNS ,
{ [Time].[1997].Children } ON ROWS
FROM [Sales_MDX1]
WHERE ( [Measures].[Unit Sales] )
```

which works fine, but does result in rather a wide grid:

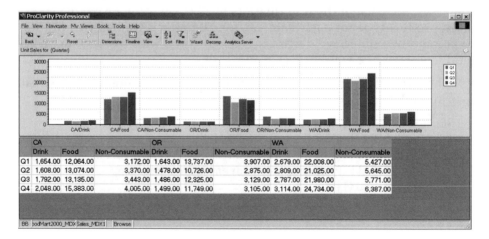

You can crossjoin on both at once:

```
SELECT
CROSSJOIN ({ [Store].[Store Country].[USA].Children } ,
{[Product].[All Products].Children}) ON COLUMNS ,
CROSSJOIN({ [Time].[1997].Children },
{[Customers].[USA].Children}) ON ROWS
FROM [Sales_MDX1]
WHERE ( [Measures].[Unit Sales] )
```

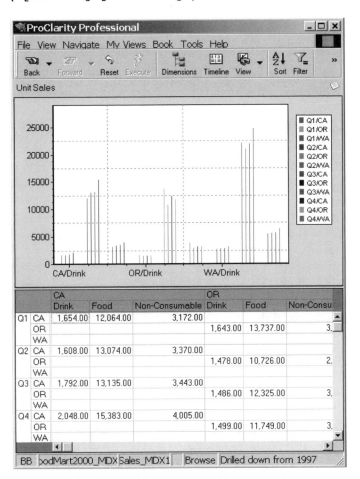

As you can see this works fine and the resulting grid proves to us that our customers only ever buy from our company in their home states.

❛ *Or, perhaps more realistically, it proves that we are using sample data...* ❜

Initially you might look at this grid of data and think "It would be really useful to eliminate those empty cells", but it turns out that in this case, you can't. The reason is that you can only eliminate completely empty rows and/or completely empty columns and, in this particular grid there aren't any rows or columns that are entirely empty; each contains at least one value somewhere. However, there are times when an MDX query will return empty rows/columns and then it can be very useful to be able to eliminate them.

NON EMPTY

In fact, empty columns/rows can be a pain even with simple MDX queries. For example:

```
SELECT
{[Customers].[All Customers].Children} ON COLUMNS,
{[Product].[All Products].Children} ON ROWS
FROM [Sales_MDX1]
```

produces a graph/grid that is mainly empty:

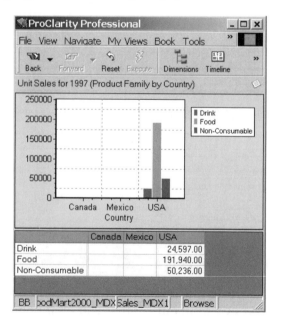

for the simple reason that there is no data in the cube for Canada or Mexico. MDX allows us to specify that we only want to see NON EMPTY columns like this:

```
SELECT
NON EMPTY {[Customers].[All Customers].Children} ON COLUMNS,
{[Product].[All Products].Children} ON ROWS
FROM [Sales_MDX1]
```

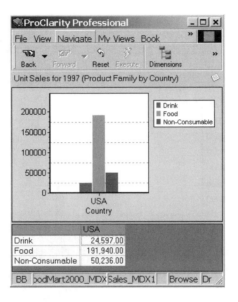

Easy or what!?

OK, try this one. Is this MDX statement going to remove the empty cells?

```
SELECT
{[Customers].[All Customers].Children} ON COLUMNS,
NON EMPTY {[Product].[All Products].Children} ON ROWS
FROM [Sales_MDX1]
```

The answer is "no" because it is only the columns that are completely empty in the original answer, not the rows. You may now be thinking "So, wouldn't something like:

```
SELECT
NON EMPTY {[Customers].[All Customers].Children} ON COLUMNS,
NON EMPTY {[Product].[All Products].Children} ON ROWS
FROM [Sales_MDX1]
```

enable me to perform a blanket removal of anything that can be removed?"

And you'd be absolutely right. This will remove whatever empty rows and columns there are.

So a query like:

```
SELECT
{[Customers].[All Customers].Children} ON COLUMNS,
{[Store].[All Stores].Children} ON ROWS
FROM [Sales_MDX1]
```

ProClarity Professional

File   View   Navigate   My Views   Book   Tools

Back   Forward   Reset   Execute   Dimensions   Timeline

Unit Sales for 1997 (Store Country by Country)

	Canada	Mexico	USA
Canada			
Mexico			
USA			266,773.00

BB bodMart2000_MDX Sales_MDX1   Browse Drilled dov

can be 'tidied up' dramatically to:

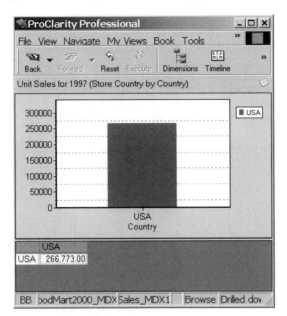

using:

```
SELECT
NON EMPTY {[Customers].[All Customers].Children} ON COLUMNS,
NON EMPTY {[Store].[All Stores].Children} ON ROWS
FROM [Sales_MDX1]
```

It is, of course, entirely a matter for you, or your users, to determine whether hiding empty cells helps or hinders the interpretation of the data. Sometimes is it vital to see the columns/rows that are empty. However, MDX does allow you to hide them when you determine that it is appropriate.

From top to bottom

Suppose that you are interested in finding out which classes of food sell best, so you use:

```
SELECT
{[Product].[Product Family].[Food].CHILDREN} ON COLUMNS
FROM [Sales_MDX1]
WHERE [Measures].[Unit Sales]
```

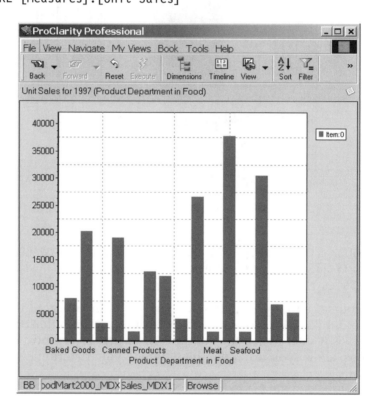

This works, after a fashion, but it is awkward to identify the top-sellers. Modifying the MDX to:

```
SELECT
{TOPCOUNT( [Product].[Product Family].[Food].CHILDREN,4,
[Measures].[Unit Sales])} ON COLUMNS
FROM [Sales_MDX1]
```

produces an output like this:

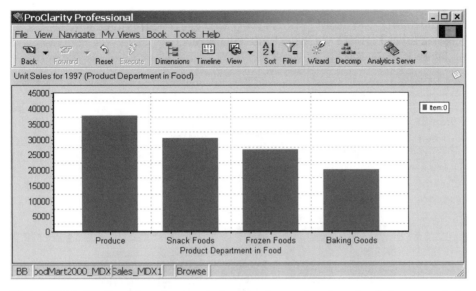

This TOPCOUNT function is worth further investigation, both because it is fundamentally useful and because we can use it to illuminate another aspect of how MDX works in general. That means that you can expect to see something weird appearing shortly.

❻ *Weird, in this instance, means something that is actually totally logical, but appears counter-intuitive at first.* ❾

TOPCOUNT takes three parameters – a set, a number and a measure:

```
{TOPCOUNT( [Product].[Product Family].[Food].CHILDREN,4,
[Measures].[Unit Sales])}
```

The function finds the four highest values of the measure Unit Sales for each of the children of the Food member. We can assume that, since we have only used products and measures to restrict the answer, this finds the top selling products for the data that is defined by the default members of the other dimensions. This is, in fact, the case, and since we will be referring to the answer of this MDX statement later, it is worth noting that the four top selling products for 1997 in All Stores and for All Customers were, in descending order:

Produce, Snack Foods, Frozen Foods, Baking Goods.

We can, of course, modify the MDX to give us the first five:

```
SELECT
{TOPCOUNT( [Product].[Product Family].[Food].CHILDREN,5,
[Measures].[Unit Sales])} ON COLUMNS
FROM [Sales_MDX1]
```

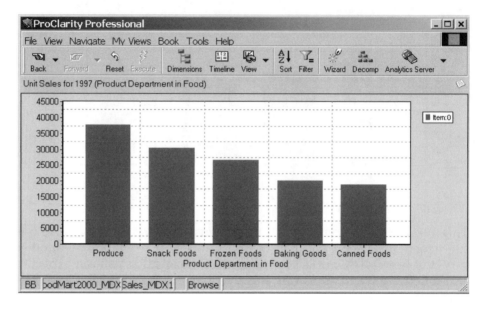

which extends our top-seller list to:

Produce, Snack Foods, Frozen Foods, Baking Goods, Canned Foods.

Nothing weird so far....

Now suppose we modify the query to read:

```
SELECT
{TOPCOUNT( [Product].[Product Family].[Food].CHILDREN,5,
[Measures].[Unit Sales])} ON COLUMNS
FROM [Sales_MDX1]
WHERE ([Store].[Store Country].[USA].[OR])
```

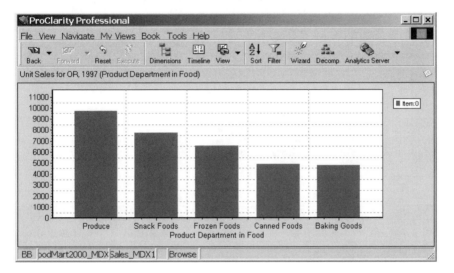

This shows us that Oregonians have buying habits that are pretty much like everyone else's, except that they happen to favor Canned Foods slightly over Baking Goods rather than the other way round. True, the figures for these two product groups are close:

Canned Foods – 4889

Baking Goods – 4810

but this still isn't weird because we'd naturally expect some variation between different states.

However, there is another way in which we could express that query, namely as:

```
SELECT
{TOPCOUNT( [Product].[Product Family].[Food].CHILDREN,5,
[Measures].[Unit Sales])} ON COLUMNS,
{[Store].[Store Country].[USA].[OR]} ON ROWS
FROM [Sales_MDX1]
```

On the face of it, this MDX statement looks as if it should return exactly the same data. After all, it uses the same sets and tuples.

❝ [Store].[Store Country].[USA].[OR] *is a tuple in the first statement and a set in the second, but that isn't the issue here.* ❞

This is where the weirdness arrives because the answer from this query is subtly different:

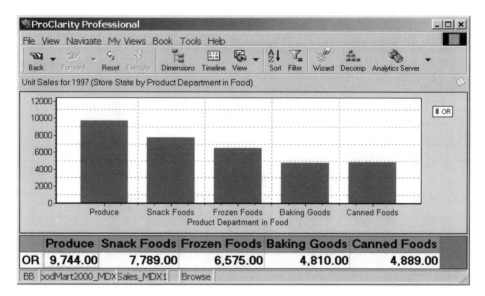

At first sight it looks as if Oregonians now prefer Baking Goods over Canned Foods; but that can't be true because the numbers are still the same as before. It's the ordering that has changed, implying that Baking Goods is the fourth most popular group rather than the fifth. But perhaps this is simply a matter of how the data is being displayed. We can test that by asking for the top four products with:

```
SELECT
{TOPCOUNT( [Product].[Product Family].[Food].CHILDREN,4,
[Measures].[Unit Sales])} ON COLUMNS,
{[Store].[Store Country].[USA].[OR]} ON ROWS
FROM [Sales_MDX1]
```

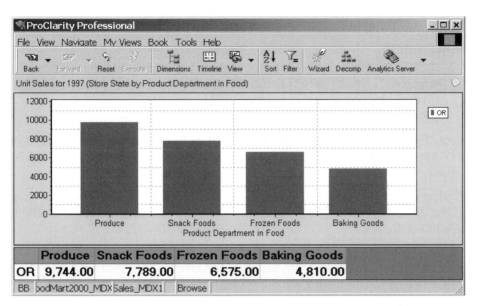

Nope, it's nothing to do with ordering. So the weirdness has arrived. This MDX query is apparently asking for the top four best-selling products in Oregon. But it clearly hasn't delivered that as an answer because we know that Canned Foods actually outsell Baking Goods in Oregon. So either Analysis Services is mis-answering the question, or we are misunderstanding exactly what this question is asking. And it turns out that the latter is true, we have misunderstood the question that this MDX statement asks.

In other words, this MDX query is asking a subtly different question from the previous one.

OK, so now we need to focus in on just what these two queries are asking.

The first one that we used to examine the buying behavior of Oregonians:

```
SELECT
{TOPCOUNT( [Product].[Product Family].[Food].CHILDREN,5,
[Measures].[Unit Sales])} ON COLUMNS
FROM [Sales_MDX1]
WHERE ([Store].[Store Country].[USA].[OR])
```

says "Find the five best-selling products in 1997 for All Customers in **the stores in Oregon** and then show me the sales figures of those five products in Oregon." Which is what it does.

❻ *Remember, the cube has four dimensions – Product, Customers, Time and Store. The default member for Time is 1997 and for Customers it is All Customers.* ❾

This second one (which on the face of it is very similar):

```
SELECT
{TOPCOUNT( [Product].[Product Family].[Food].CHILDREN,5,
[Measures].[Unit Sales])} ON COLUMNS,
{[Store].[Store Country].[USA].[OR]} ON ROWS
FROM [Sales_MDX1]
```

says "Find the top five best-selling products in 1997 for All Customers in **All Stores** and then show me the sales figures of those five products in Oregon." Which is what **it** does.

And, of course, both of these questions are perfectly valid ways of looking at the data, and so MDX has to have a way to allow you to ask both – which is what it does.

So now we have two different types of question we can ask about top sellers, but what you need to know is the overall rule that tells us which construction to use under what circumstances.

And the answer is that it all comes down to the difference between an axis like ROWS and the WHERE clause.

If something like:

```
([Store].[Store Country].[USA].[OR])
```

appears in a WHERE clause, then it is used to restrict the data that is pulled back from the cube. If it appears in an ON ROWS clause, it is simply used to determine how the data should be laid out for the user.

Now, in many cases, this distinction is not vital. For example, consider a simple query like this:

```
SELECT
{[Time].[1997].[Q1]} ON COLUMNS
FROM [Sales_MDX1]
WHERE ( [Measures].[Unit Sales] )
```

The WHERE clause means that the MDX statement is only ever going to work with data from the Unit Sales measure.

The:

```
{[Time].[1997].[Q1]} ON COLUMNS
```

clause means that the MDX statement is only ever going to display the data for the first quarter of 1997. In this case there is very little functional difference between the two.

In fact, you can reverse the tuples/sets to give:

```
SELECT
{[Measures].[Unit Sales] }ON COLUMNS
FROM [Sales_MDX1]
WHERE ([Time].[1997].[Q1])
```

which gives the same result – 66,291 units sold of All Products to All Customers in All Stores for the first quarter on 1997.

However, in the case of our two 'weird' MDX queries, the difference is vital.

In the first:

```
SELECT
{TOPCOUNT( [Product].[Product Family].[Food].CHILDREN,5,
[Measures].[Unit Sales])} ON COLUMNS
FROM [Sales_MDX1]
WHERE ([Store].[Store Country].[USA].[OR])
```

the WHERE clause is ensuring that the TOPCOUNT function only operates on the data from Oregon.

In the second:

```
SELECT
{TOPCOUNT( [Product].[Product Family].[Food].CHILDREN,5,
[Measures].[Unit Sales])} ON COLUMNS,
{[Store].[Store Country].[USA].[OR]} ON ROWS
FROM [Sales_MDX1]
```

there is no WHERE clause to restrict the TOPCOUNT function to just data from the Oregon stores, and the ON ROWS clause is simply controlling the way the data is laid out.

So use the WHERE clause to control which data TOPCOUNT is using to find the top values.

Now that was reasonably heavy stuff (if you are new to it) so to lighten it up a little, we'll introduce you to BOTTOMCOUNT which does exactly as the name suggests. So:

```
SELECT
{BOTTOMCOUNT( [Product].[Product Family].[Food].CHILDREN,2,
[Measures].[Unit Sales])} ON COLUMNS,
{[Store].[Store Country].[USA].Children} ON ROWS
FROM [Sales_MDX1]
```

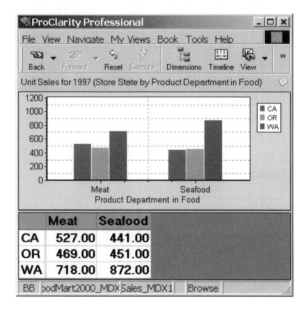

shows you that the worst selling product group overall is Meat.

And, just because we can't resist stressing the point (one last time, honest) about the difference between ON ROWS and WHERE, what would you guess that the following will do?

```
SELECT
{BOTTOMCOUNT( [Product].[Product Family].[Food].CHILDREN,2,
[Measures].[Unit Sales])} ON COLUMNS,
{[Store].[Store Country].[USA].Children} ON ROWS
FROM [Sales_MDX1]
WHERE ([Customers].[State Province].[OR])
```

Look away from your book now and press the 'mute' button on your remote if you want to guess before seeing the result...

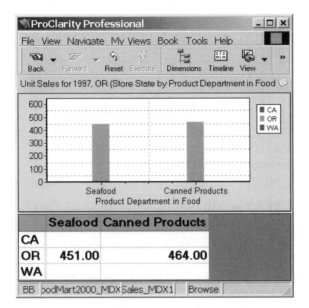

Not only has the WHERE clause excluded any results for CA or WA, one of the products ranked in the bottom two has actually changed because Oregonians, once more, differ slightly from the herd.

More than two dimensions – PAGES, SECTIONS, CHAPTERS

In MDX, the ON COLUMNS and ON ROWS clauses specify how your data appears on a grid with two axes – the columns forming one axis and the rows the second. But suppose that you want to slice by more than two dimensions. In that case you can specify up to three additional axes by name: PAGES, SECTIONS and CHAPTERS.

We can add one axis at a time to a simple MDX query:

```
SELECT
{[Customers].[All Customers].[USA].Children} ON COLUMNS,
{[Product].[All Products].Children} ON ROWS,
{[Time].[1998].Children} ON PAGES
FROM [Sales_MDX1]
```

```
SELECT
{[Customers].[All Customers].[USA].Children} ON COLUMNS,
{[Product].[All Products].Children} ON ROWS,
{[Time].[1998].Children} ON PAGES,
{[Store],[USA].Children} ON SECTIONS
FROM [Sales_MDX1]
```

```
SELECT
{[Customers].[All Customers].[USA].Children} ON COLUMNS,
{[Product].[All Products].Children} ON ROWS,
{[Time].[1998].Children} ON PAGES,
{[Store],[USA].Children} ON SECTIONS,
{[Measures].Members} ON CHAPTERS
FROM [Sales_MDX1]
```

A couple of points are worth noting about the use of axes.

These are the only five names (or aliases) that you can use to specify dimensions. What if you need more? Well, you can specify up to 128, but for that you have to use an alternative naming convention which is numerically based. You can specify axes by number – AXIS(0) for columns, AXIS(1) for rows, AXIS(2) for pages, AXIS(3) for sections and AXIS(4) for chapters, AXIS(5) for the next one, AXIS(6) for the next and so on up to AXIS(127).

```
SELECT
{[Customers].[All Customers].[USA].Children} ON AXIS(0),
{[Product].[All Products].Children} ON AXIS(1),
{[Time].[1998].Children} ON AXIS(2),
{[Store],[USA].Children} ON AXIS(3),
{[Measures].Members} ON AXIS(4)
FROM [Sales_MDX1]
```

In fact, in Analysis Services, you can even shorten this to:

```
SELECT
{[Customers].[All Customers].[USA].Children} ON 0,
{[Product].[All Products].Children} ON 1,
{[Time].[1998].Children} ON 2,
{[Store],[USA].Children} ON 3,
{[Measures].Members} ON 4
FROM [Sales_MDX1]
```

You can even mix and match:

```
SELECT
{[Customers].[All Customers].[USA].Children} ON AXIS(0),
{[Product].[All Products].Children} ON AXIS(1),
{[Time].[1998].Children} ON 2,
{[Store],[USA].Children} ON SECTIONS,
{[Measures].Members} ON AXIS(4)
FROM [Sales_MDX1]
```

What you can't do, no matter which naming convention you use, is to mess around with the order in which the names appear. Neither can you skip an axis so, for example, you can't leave out Sections and still specify Chapters.

When logic and people collide...

You'll notice that we haven't used any screen shots from ProClarity to show a graphical interpretation of this data. The reason is simple: if you cut and paste these MDX queries into ProClarity, the user interface doesn't display the full set of data.

Now the obvious interpretation is that this is a bug; but it turns out that it isn't a bug – it's a feature. No, really. It is a feature based on the several years of experience that ProClarity as a company has gained about how users interact with data coming back from cubes. For example, for many users the combination of multi-dimensional slicing of data with filtering tends to produce counter-intuitive results.

That's what the people at ProClarity say and one of the reasons that we believe them is that earlier versions of ProClarity did display this data on screen, using combo boxes to represent the extra dimensions. The company has actually taken the functionality out because it was causing grief for users.

Of course, none of the authors of this book works for ProClarity so we haven't seen the actual feedback from users that has precipitated this change, but we know someone who has – Russ Whitney. Not only is he the Vice President of Research & Development for ProClarity, he is also a contributing editor for *SQL Server Magazine*, where he writes the MDX column, Mastering Analysis.

Russ Whitney says:

MDX is a very powerful query language. Much of that power comes from MDX's multi-dimensional nature. With a language like SQL you are inherently limited to rows and columns; functions like sorting, grouping and filtering are tied to items

that are on the rows. This is not true about MDX. You can sort and filter columns just as easily as you can rows. Also, you can include more dimensions in your query result than just rows and columns. With MDX you can call out these other dimensions by their names like pages, sections and chapters or you can just refer to them by index like Axis(2), Axis(3), etc.

Although all this power is nice, it doesn't change the fact that analysts and business decision makers think in terms of rows and columns. In addition, most analytic tools present data in a two-dimensional manner. Even MDX recognizes this by implying a certain presentation in the syntax. For example, the names pages, sections and chapters imply a book-style presentation where there is a grid of rows and columns on each page.

Unfortunately what we have found in practice is that there is a conflict between the pure and orthogonal way that MDX handles n-dimensional results and the way that most users would expect to have them work in a two-dimensional world. The best way to demonstrate this is through an example. Let's take the ever present FoodMart 2000 Sales cube and run a 3 dimensional query and look at the results.

```
Select [Time].[1997].Children on Columns,
Non Empty [Customers].[All Customers].[USA].[OR].
Children on Rows,
Descendants([Store].[All Stores].[USA].[OR], [Store].[Store
Name]) on Pages
from Sales
```

This query displays total unit sales for each quarter of 1997 for each city in Oregon. The query is paged by each store in Oregon. Furthermore, I have requested that empty customer cities be eliminated. The result for the first store name (e.g. the first page) is shown below.

	Q1	Q2	Q3	Q4
Albany				
Beaverton	1,107.00	1,374.00	852.00	1,225.00
Corvallis				
Lake Oswego	1,102.00	1,310.00	1,003.00	1,495.00
Lebanon				
Milwaukie	1,345.00	1,279.00	1,295.00	1,226.00
Oregon City	1,113.00	815.00	888.00	892.00
Portland	1,001.00	940.00	676.00	966.00
Salem				
W. Linn	1,041.00	1,134.00	777.00	1,223.00
Woodburn				

So if I requested to have empty customer cities to be eliminated, why do Albany, Corvallis, Lebanon, Salem and Woodburn still show up? The reason is that MDX treats rows the same as any other dimension. What I mean by that is that the keyword Non Empty applies to all other dimensions returned in the result. In order for

Albany to be considered empty it would have to be empty on all columns and all pages. In this example, some of the pages contain data for Albany and some don't.

This same effect applies to all types of sorting and filtering in MDX. Let's say you wanted to see the top 10 customers for each state. It might seem like pages is an obvious way to separate each state.

```
Select {[Unit Sales]} on Columns,
TopCount( [Customers].[Name].Members, 10,
[Unit Sales] ) on Rows,
[Store].[Store State].Members on Pages
from Sales
```

This query returns the following result for the first state:

	Unit Sales
Mary Francis Benigar	
Wildon Cameron	
Ida Rodriguez	
James Horvat	
Joann Mramor	
Kristin Miller	
Matt Bellah	
George Todero	
Jack Zucconi	
Frank Darrell	

How can the top 10 customers have no Unit Sales? The answer is that there is no way for each page to have a different set of rows (or a different order for the rows). MDX determines the top 10 customers overall and displays the unit sales for each state on each page.

This MDX behavior would be more intuitive if the result was displayed in 3 dimensions. For example, a 3d bar chart or a 3d scatter chart. But what happens when you need to display a 4 dimensional result? It can be done through color or other attributes but charts like this are very difficult to read.

Because of the issues described here, ProClarity chose not to use the pages, sections, chapters and other axis possible in MDX queries. If you request a paged result in ProClarity (we call it a slicer) we execute an independent 2 dimension query for each change. This ensures that filtering and sorting in combination with "paging" to work as most users would expect.

In essence this means that ProClarity allows you to create a user interface that will let you see the top ten customers for each state. While this is not a

'Teach you how to use ProClarity' book, in this one instance it seems worth showing you how.

Open the Sales cube from FoodMart 2000. Open the dimensions pane, drag Measures into the Columns box (bottom of the screen) and then use the tabbed area at the top of the screen to select Measures and make sure that Unit Sales is selected.

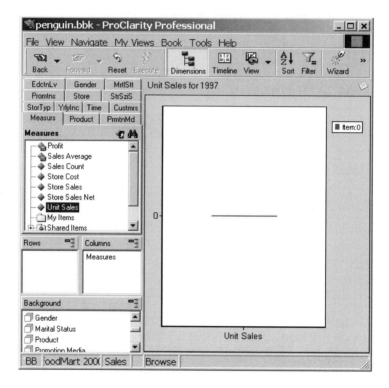

Then add Customers to the Rows box, select the Customers tab, right click on All Customers and make the following selection:

Now click on the Filter button and in the Advanced tab, set up the following:

To take care of the third axis, find Store in the Background box, right click on it and select as shown:

and then go to the Store tab, right click on All Stores and select as follows:

As you select each state from the combo box, you see what users seem to intuitively expect, which is the top ten customers from each state.

❻ *Note that data only exists for CA, WA and OR.* **❾**

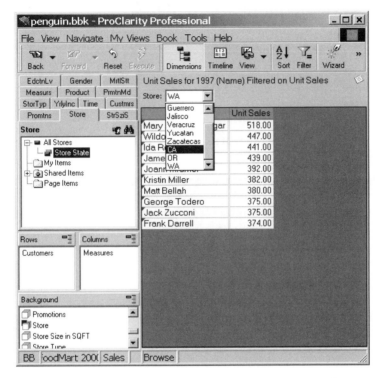

Every time you make a selection from the combo box, ProClarity is generating a new MDX statement for the particular selection you make and sends that to the cube. You can, of course, use the MDX editor to see that MDX.

For WA it looks like this:

```
SELECT
{ [Measures].[Unit Sales] } ON COLUMNS ,
{ TOPCOUNT( { DESCENDANTS( [Customers].[All Customers],
[Customers].[Name] ) }, 10, ( [Measures].[Unit Sales] ) ) }
ON ROWS
FROM [Sales]
WHERE ( [Store].[Store State].&[WA] )
```

For CA, like this:

```
SELECT
{ [Measures].[Unit Sales] } ON COLUMNS ,
{ TOPCOUNT( { DESCENDANTS( [Customers].[All Customers],
[Customers].[Name] ) }, 10, ( [Measures].[Unit Sales] ) ) }
ON ROWS
FROM [Sales]
WHERE ( [Store].[Store State].&[CA] )
```

Summary

There's a range of additional features that you can add to MDX queries, the main ones are covered here.

In addition, it is worth remembering that MDX is a rigorous language that abides by a precise and logical set (if you'll pardon the expression) of rules. The better you understand how MDX works, the more you can use its power.

Summary of the book

We hope you get as much fun out of MDX as we, in our various ways, have already done.

Appendix 1

Sample files

Where and what are the sample files?

There is a folder in the root directory of the CD-ROM called `MDXBook` and in here you'll find three types of file:

`.CAB`
`.MDB`
`.TXT`

CAB files

A `.CAB` file is the standard archiving format that Analysis Services uses to back up databases. It contains everything required in order to rebuild an Analysis Services database. When you restore a `.CAB` file with Analysis Services, the result is a database containing one or more cubes. Given a standard installation of Analysis Services, all the files pertaining to both database and cubes will be located, after restoration, in `C:\Program Files\Microsoft Analysis Services\Data\`*DatabaseName*; but your mileage may vary.

If you have been using Analysis Services for any length of time it is highly likely that you know how to restore these files using Analysis Manager, but just in case you don't we've included a step-by-step guide to the process below. However, before you restore them, please bear in mind that these databases are not meant to represent real operational OLAP cubes. There are quite a few of them and they have often been developed to illustrate a particular point, so they are not necessarily examples of good overall OLAP cube design. In addition, they have not been rigorously checked out to ensure that they will not interfere with existing operational systems so they are provided without any guarantees at all. We recommend that you install them on a test system, preferably on a stand-alone machine; we actively discourage you from installing them on an operational server.

Many of the chapters in this book contain practical examples and we encourage you to work through them. In case you have any problems, we have also supplied five .CAB files which contain the completed practical work at different stages through the book. So if you get stuck at any point, you can always restore the relevant completed database to see a working example. The only point to bear in mind is that restoring from these .CAB files will create databases of the same name as the originals and which will, of course, overwrite them. So if you have already completed any work you might want to create an archive of that **before** restoring from one of our sample .CAB files.

MDB files

When restored from its .CAB file, each database will be pointing to a data source file containing the original data from which the cube is derived. The .MDB files (Microsoft Access format) on the CD-ROM contain this data.

TXT files

In the same folder you will also find a series of text files called, for example, CHAP8.TXT. These contain all of the MDX queries and/or expressions that we have used in the appropriate chapter. They are there so that you try the MDX for yourself by cutting and pasting it into any front-end tool that you want to use – for example, ProClarity.

When to use which files

At the start of each chapter we name the .CAB file that you need to restore in order to work through the examples, the cube you'll need and the .CAB file you can restore if you want to see the completed examples. Finally, we tell you where the MDX samples are located. For example, the resources for Chapter 5 are:

Starting database – FoodMart2000_MDX1
Cube – Sales_MDX1
Completed sample database – FoodMart2000_EndChap7.CAB
MDX samples – CHAP5.TXT

How to manage the files

As we said above, all of these files are on the CD-ROM in a folder called MDXBook. Since these are on a CD-ROM they are, of course, read-only, so you'll need to copy them to a hard disk somewhere before you start.

We recommend that you copy all of the files in this folder to your PC; not only that, we highly recommend that you create a folder called MDXBook in the root of drive C:\ and place the files in there (in other words, in a folder called C:\MDXBook).

Now this may all sound a little control-freakish of us and of course you are free to put the files wherever you like. However, the reason we are so specific about location has to do with the relationship between an OLAP cube and its original source of data.

When you create an OLAP cube you obviously have to supply it with a source of data, and so the cube stores a pointer to that data source. If you create a .CAB file from an OLAP cube, then that .CAB file also includes the same pointer information. So it follows that when you restore a .CAB file, that self-same pointer is restored. Now, we are supplying you with a set of .CAB files, so when you restore from them you are also restoring all of those pointers. When we built the .CAB files we did so from a folder called C:\MDXBook so if you use the same folder on your machine, you should be able to restore any .CAB file and it will be able to locate and use the correct data file.

If you find that you want/have to use another folder name, then you can still use the instructions in the rest of this appendix; simply substitute the folder name of your choosing. Once the databases have been restored from the .CAB files, you'll have to manually reset the pointer to the new location of the data source. This is described below in the section headed "Data Sources".

Step-by-step guide to restoring an Analysis Service Database (containing one or more OLAP cubes) from a .CAB file

We'll assume that you have copied the files from the CD-ROM to a folder called C:\MDXBook. Since the files have been copied from a CD-ROM, they will be marked as read-only in the folder on your machine. Highlight all of the files in C:\MDXBook, right click and uncheck the box labelled Read-only.

253

Fire up Analysis Services and in the Analysis Manager tree pane, right click on the server to which the database is going to be restored and choose the 'Restore Database' option.

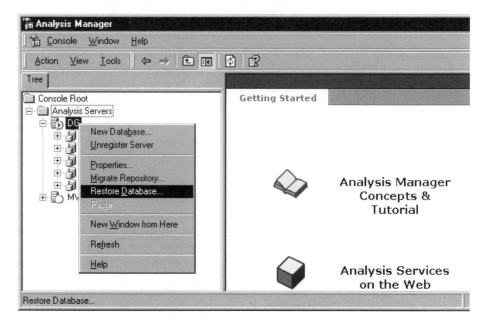

Navigate to the appropriate .CAB file.

Confirm that you want to perform the restore.

Restore Database	☒
Server:	DG
Database name:	FoodMart2000_MDX1
File Information:	60 files; 5,497KB
Restore from:	C:\MDXBook\FoodMart2000_MDX1.CAB
Archive date:	21/08/01 10:37:53

Restore	Cancel	Help

Watch the process proceed before your eyes and finally click on the close button.

Restore Database Progress ☒

60 of 60 files; 5,497KB of 5,497KB

- File: Sales_MDX1A.3.fact.map (46KB)
- File: Sales_MDX1A.pdr (0.0KB)
- File: OLAPDB.REP (43KB)
- Updating repository.
- Updating DSO.
- Validating roles.
- Processing security for cube: Sales_MDX1
- Processing security for cube: Sales_MDX1A
- ✓ Database successfully restored.

Save Log ...	Close	Help

It really should be that simple and it has been when we've tried it. If we find that people are having any problems with the files on the CD-ROM, we'll post help on the website:

www.penguinsoft.co.uk

Data sources

As we have said, databases in Analysis Services point to a data source file
(which can be an Access .MDB file, as is the case for ours, or whatever). If you
get a message when you try to edit a cube that says the data source cannot
be accessed, or if you have put the files in a location other then C:\MDXBook,
then you'll need to check that the pointer to the location of the data source
is correct. To do this, right click on the data source for the cube, choose Edit:

and the Data Link Properties dialog opens. In the Connections tab, under 'Select or enter a database name', check that this is pointing to the correct file and edit it if not.

Appendix 2

ProClarity

Installing ProClarity and connecting it to a cube

Place the CD-ROM into the drive on your computer and it should automatically run the ProClarity setup software. If it doesn't, inspect the contents of the CD-ROM, find the file called SETUP.EXE and click on it to run it. A dialog opens up which allows you to see the documentation, which includes the system requirements and an extensive Getting Started guide. It also allows you to install ProClarity if you so desire.

When ProClarity is fired up, it first asks you what you want to open. Select 'Cube for browsing' and click OK.

![Screenshot of the ProClarity Welcome dialog box. Title bar reads "Welcome..." with help and close buttons. The heading shows "ProClarity® Analytics Platform 5 Professional". Text: "Analyze and share data via the Web - make decisions with ProClarity!" with "ProClarity Web Site" link. Under "Open" section are radio buttons: "ProClarity Analytics Server", "Cube for browsing" (selected), "Local briefing book", "Briefing book from ProClarity Analytics Server" (greyed out). A list area with columns Book, Library, Server. Buttons at bottom: OK, Cancel, Help, About.]

Now identify the server where your cube sits and click OK.

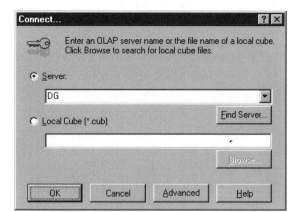

Navigate to the cube you want, highlight it and click OK.

The last question is how you wish to view your data; it doesn't matter too much what you pick here as once you're looking at the data you can swop between representations very easily and at will.

Select how you want to visualize your information.

    Chart View

    Decomposition Tree

    Perspective

    Grid

☑ Use as default view

If you want to choose a view to use as the default, click the 'Use as default view' box before you make a selection. Next time you open ProClarity, you won't see this step and your data will automatically be shown in your chosen view.

ProClarity also supplies various pieces of documentation about the software and how to use it. For a basic get-you-going guide, check out the file entitled `GettingStartedGuide.pdf`; you can navigate to it from the installation software or simply search for it on the CD-ROM.

Using ProClarity's MDX Editor

To open ProClarity's MDX editor, click View on the main menu and select 'MDX Editor'.

The top pane is where you construct MDX code. You can either type it in or build it by making selections from the panes below where you'll find the hierarchy of the cube with all its members on the left and the whole range of MDX functions, categorized by type, on the right.

You can check the accuracy of your code with the 'Test MDX' button, Format it into lines of code (so that it's more readable than when shown as one long string) and finally Execute it.

Index